ADVANCE PRAISE

"In the nearly 40 years that I have known Gilbert Martina, I have seen them grow as an authority in the field and become an extraordinary CEO and leader. Their leadership is characterized by not only a business perspective but also by considering mental health and the context of health in historical contexts and social realities. They connect the past, present, and future with an offer of hope. Gilbert is inspiring and decisive. This book is a must for anyone who wants to think about new leadership."

—JOHN LEERDAM, DIRECTOR OF THE SLAVERY
MUSEUM IN AMSTERDAM, NETHERLANDS

"I have had the privilege of witnessing Gilbert Martina's journey as a modern medicine-man in his training at The Four Winds Society. Gilbert embodies the qualities of perseverance, humility, charisma, and a deep integrity and dedication to healing the world, which shines through in his work. In Healthy Minds, Healthy Nation, he invites us to discover the wisdom within ourselves and to recognize how meditation and shamanic practices can bring positive transformation not only to the individual but to our communities and the world. This is a relevant and timely book, written by a man who has walked the path of spirit with courage and authenticity. I keep Gilbert's book by my bedside and am honored to endorse his work and vision."

—ALBERTO VILLOLDO, PHD, FOUNDER, THE FOUR WINDS SOCIETY

"Gilbert Martina walks the path of wisdom with humility, integrity, and an open heart. In *Healthy Minds, Healthy Nation*, he offers a map for healing that reminds us how personal transformation can radiate outward to uplift communities and nations."

—MARCELA LOBOS, AUTHOR OF *THE SACRED ANDEAN CODES* AND LEAD FACULTY AT THE FOUR WINDS SOCIETY

"*Healthy Minds, Healthy Nation* is a compelling manifesto that demonstrates how healthy minds form the foundation of strong, resilient societies. Martina—both in person and through this book—inspires entire communities to collaborate and achieve lasting success with his remarkable ability to connect and persevere."

—ATILAY USLU, FOUNDER OF THE CORENDON GROUP OF COMPANIES

"As a healthcare CEO, Gilbert Martina led the team that realised the most modern hospital of the Caribbean, the Curaçao Medical Center. Under his leadership, the center played a major role in battling the COVID pandemic. With this wealth of experience in modern healthcare and crisis management, Gilbert, with this book, tells the story of why ancient knowledge matters to the modern world."

—ERNST KUIPERS, FORMER MINISTER OF HEALTH, WELFARE, AND SPORT, FORMER CEO OF ERASMUS UNIVERSITY MEDICAL CENTER, ROTTERDAM, THE NETHERLANDS, AND PROFESSOR OF GASTROENTEROLOGY

HEALTHY MINDS, HEALTHY NATION

Healthy Minds, Healthy Nation

How Meditation, Shamanism, *and* Indigenous Healing Can Tap *into* Your Light Within *and* Change *the* World

GILBERT MARTINA

HEALTHY MINDS, HEALTHY NATION
*How Meditation, Shamanism, and Indigenous Healing Can
Tap into Your Light Within and Change the World*

FIRST EDITION

ISBN   978-1-5445-5026-8   *Hardcover*
       978-1-5445-5025-1   *Paperback*
       978-1-5445-5027-5   *Ebook*

Thank you, Dad, for your love, your kindness, your charisma, and the joy you shared through cooking and music. Your spirit lives on in every memory, and you will be forever in my heart."

Thank you, Mom, for your love, discipline, your service-mindedness, and the strength of your principles. Your legacy guides me, and you will be forever in my heart.

Contents

BECOMING THE LIGHT

Everywhere is light.
Everywhere is energy.
Who are we, really?
Where do we belong?
Why have we come?

Everywhere is light.
Everywhere is love.
Where are we going?
What must we release?
What truth must we remember?

Everywhere is light.
Everywhere is hope.
What will we become
When we stop running
And start healing?
Let us forgive the past.
Let us make space—
For the present,
For the future,
For all we are becoming.

Let us grow through the cracks.
Let us rise from the pain.
Let us shed the skin.
Let us open our hearts.
Let us be the light—
Because healing begins with us.
Because hope begins within.

—BY CHANTAL MARTINA SEFERINA

Introduction

Despite having been separated for thirty-eight years, my parents passed away within six months of each other—my father on February 4, 2023, and my mother on August 10, 2023. It felt like my father's death triggered my mother's; two weeks after his passing, she was admitted to the hospital with acute abdominal pain. Two surgeries later, she stopped eating. They died in the same palliative center, in the same room, and in the same bed.

Although I found solace that I could be with both my father and my mother during their last moments and assist them in transitioning from the physical world to the spiritual world, I wondered what I would do without my father's wisdom and my mother's mission of service. My father carried the collective knowledge of our ancestors from the countryside of our island of Curaçao: agriculture, goats, sheep farming, and astrology, along with his passion for cooking and music. My mother was the Mother Teresa of our family, always there to help anyone who needed emotional, spiritual, or any other kind of support. Now, at age fifty-one, I was parentless.

I am certain my mother and father departed this world for a greater purpose. They transcended a physical presence and are now omnipresent, completely united as a couple and integrated into the spiritual world. I received confirmation of this during my yearly spiritual retreat on the island of Mykonos, Greece. In September 2023, while experiencing a vision quest, I asked my mother and father where they were, and my mother answered in her native language, *"Mi yu, nos ta tur kaminda"* ("My son, we are everywhere"). My instructions were clear: I should carry this ancestral wisdom and her Mother Teresa traits forward.

Still, it was after my parents' deaths that I realized my body had been suffering for a long time. I had been experiencing chronic lower-back pain since 2004, just one year after returning to Curaçao from living in the Netherlands for sixteen years. On the physical level, the pain was caused by a herniated disk at the L5-S1 level on the right side, which compressed a nerve and caused radiating pain in my right leg. I underwent three surgeries in 2005, 2007, and 2011 to address the issue. But this was more than physical pain—it was spiritual pain, and it became evident when two spiritual retreats in Abadjania, Brazil, alleviated my chronic physical pain.

What happens when life squeezes you? What happens when you experience suffering? You may feel like you haven't found the people who truly accept and understand you. It's like your personhood is being challenged, like your grief or trauma are too much to bear, like you won't survive an injury or ailment, but these experiences can be gifts that help you identify the areas where you need to improve.

Our minds can either heal us or harm us. When we face physical, emotional, and spiritual pain, we have a choice. We can succumb to the dark thoughts that victimize us, or we can tap into the light within. In the words of Pierre Teilhard de Chardin, "We are not human beings in search of a spiritual experience, but we are spiritual beings immersed in a human life."

MY TRANSFORMATIVE JOURNEY

Healing my mind didn't begin with my parents' deaths, however. In 2010, after a season of sleepless nights worrying about how I was going to steer my employer, ENNIA, out of a host of solvency issues, I searched for methods to calm the mind. I found transcendental meditation provided immediate relief. I realized the issues ENNIA was facing were relative, but my mind made a statement that they were absolute.

Then in 2016, I discovered shamanism and indigenous healing through Dr. Alberto Villoldo, a medical anthropologist. He lived and learned from the shamans of South America for more than twenty-five years. I started with his books—*Shaman, Healer, Sage, One Spirit Medicine,* and *Grow a New Body*—which show how spirit and power plants can transform your health. I traveled to Los Lobos, Chile, in February 2017 for the retreat "Grow a New Body." It was a life-transforming experience. I gained insight and strength from the ancient teachings about shamanism combined with science.

Over the years, to alleviate my stress, I turned to wisdom teachers from the past, such as Marcus Aurelius Antoninus, Mahatma Gandhi, Maharishi Mahesh Yogi, and Dr. Alberto Villoldo from the present. Marcus Aurelius, a Roman emperor from 161 to 180 AD and a Stoic philosopher, once said, "The nearer a man comes to a calm mind, the closer he is to strength." Gandhi, an Indian lawyer, anti-colonial nationalist and political ethicist, advised, "Watch your thoughts, they become words. Watch your words, they become actions. Watch your actions, they become habits. Watch your habits, they become character and watch your character, for it becomes your destiny." A calm mind is a mind free of anger, fear, jealousy, greed, pain, and worry. Such a mind comes closer to its true strength.

If you have ever taken a weekend meditation retreat or even walked in nature, you know the mind can still be preoccupied with thoughts about endless to-do lists and unresolved situations. We all have or can recognize these lists: I have to buy groceries, I have to cook, the children have appointments. All the action points to work; all our worries, desires, personal exercise goals, and so on. It is difficult to quiet our minds and focus on the present moment. The mind is often preoccupied with unfinished business from the past, worries about the future, or desires for what is to come.

The mind can be compared to the ocean, which is active on the surface but calm and still deep down. Our mind can be active on the surface while still deep. This is what Marcus Aurelius referred to when he mentioned that a calm mind brings us closer to our true potential, the voice of our soul, rather than our ego.

When an extended professional crisis at my old employer, ENNIA, took hold of me, for example, leaving me with endless sleepless nights, all I could think about was that the foundation of the insurance business is all about trust. I trust the insurance company will pay my non-life insurance claims if an unforeseen incident occurs: sickness, car accident, fire, earthquake, or hurricane. In addition, I trust the insurance company will pay my scheduled pension benefit when I reach retirement age. Jeopardizing an insurance company's mission is a violation of trust. All the financial indicators: asset liability management, solvency calculation, and liquidity projections indicated there would be a problem in the future. Everything in my body was protesting.

These questions were taking a mental, emotional, and spiritual toll. My mind played an unhealthy loop of tape, over and over: What was the intention of the shareholder who had invested premiums of pension policyholders in his affiliated companies? Ultimately, in an October 2022 court ruling, there would be justice, but at the time, it shattered my view of the company for which I worked and the corporate and nation-state in which I was immersed. Was I trapped in the so-called golden cage?

Even in the darkest hours, there are seeds of hope. I look back now, and I remember that I developed a presentation for ENNIA's Prevent Now seminars, held at the World Trade Center of Curaçao. Its title? "Healthy Minds for a Healthy Nation." That was the seed of this book—*Healthy Minds, Healthy Nation: How Meditation, Shamanism, and Indigenous Healing Can Tap into Your Light Within and Change the World.*

HEALTHY MINDS, HEALTHY NATIONS

Healthy Minds, Healthy Nation is a book about tapping into the light within, even in difficult circumstances. It emphasizes the importance of self-reflection and personal growth. I will share my experience with physical pain and suffering and how it led to a realization that these challenges are opportunities for growth. I hope this book will guide you in striving for a healthier mind and a healthier society (nation) and world. I aim to introduce you to transcendental meditation, shamanism, and indigenous healing as ways to transform your consciousness.

Healthy Minds, Healthy Nation will take you on a journey through the teachings of transcendental meditation from Maharishi Mahesh Yogi, as well as teachings about how to tap the light within in times of great turbulence, using energy-healing practices from ancient South American and Curaçao wisdom featuring Dr. Alberto Villoldo and Marcela Lobos. In the pages ahead, you will see how you can integrate transcendental meditation and ancient energy healing wisdom into your daily life, even in, and especially during, turbulent times.

Many of these teachings have been around for thousands of years, but most people in the Western world have ignored them because we have become disconnected from what truly matters in our daily lives. We have created a world based on power, ego, and fear instead of a world based on unconditional love. We were all humans until race disconnected us, religion separated us, wealth classified us, and politics divided us. The separation takes place in our minds, creating unhealthy states of mind, because on a spiritual level, we are spiritual beings having a human experience. We are beings of light, beings of love. We have an opportunity now to practice unconditional love daily, and I want to show you the way.

Can one have a calm mind when it is filled with information from past, present, and even future desires, as well as traumas from childhood and past lives? The answer is yes. I have seen and experienced it myself.

I have talked about cultivating a healthy mind, but I also want you to see that we can create healthy nations if we have healthy minds. In this book, I examine the systems that shape our lives. I ask questions such as, "What is the impact of slavery on its modern-day descendants? How can individuals release traumas from their current or past lives?"

For example, as a native of the island of Curaçao, once a colony of the Netherlands, now an autonomous nation within the Kingdom of the Netherlands, I know Curaçao played a central role in the transatlantic transportation of slaves. In these pages, I'll discuss the historical perspective of Curaçao, including the ancient native inhabitants, the Spanish, Portuguese, and Dutch colonial periods, the introduction of slavery under Dutch rule, the relationship with Africa due to slavery, and its implications for modern society. Having emigrated to the Netherlands to study, I worked as an executive director, suffered from lower-back pain, and gained awareness through transcendental meditation, shamanism, and indigenous healing. I bring a grounded understanding of the effects of ancient native traditions and the long history of slavery on modern society.

All of us are living in a world today where we can observe actions of unhealthy minds and unconscious behavior around us. We are in the soup that humanity has created over the past decades and centuries. A masculine perspective of the world, based on power over others, rules how we live and die, compared to a more feminine perspective, which is the core of Mother Earth, or *Pachamama*, as it is called in Quechua. We are shifting from an egocentric to an altruistic perspective of the world.

Why do we have so much suffering around the world? Why do we have so many wars now? As of this writing, Russia and Ukraine have been fighting since the invasion of Russia on February 24, 2022. The war in Gaza has, of course, also cost many lives. Closer to home, in Venezuela, there is significant social unrest. The current president,

Nicoláas Maduro, who was elected on April 14, 2013, was captured on January 3, 2026 and jailed in New York for narco-terrorism. Many Venezuelans have been migrating to other South and Central American countries, and even in Curaçao, we have seen an influx of Venezuelan immigrants.

According to *The Washington Post*, there have been 714 school shootings since 1999 in America, and more than 383,000 students have experienced gun violence at school since Columbine. Can you imagine taking your children to school every day and having to deal with the fear of hearing on the news that there has been a shooting at your children's school and having the question of whether your child is among the victims?

What are the root causes of all the unhealthy minds that are causing all these sufferings around the world? How can we deal with this root cause to create a better world for our future generations?

Healthy Minds, Healthy Nation teaches all of us how to develop a calm mind and heal ourselves and our nations. The focus is on teaching how to develop a calm mind and heal traumas from past and current lives using ancient healing techniques from the Americas. The book covers spiritual growth, consciousness, and the practice of unconditional love to create beauty for individuals willing to make the transition from a human being to a human luminous. Every human being can be a source of light for others without diminishing their own light. Unconditional love and happiness only increase when shared.

Part I

A Foundation for a Healthy Mind

CHAPTER 1

The Importance of Guiding Principles

Before you can do the work of developing a healthy mind, let alone fighting injustice and inequality in your nation, you must establish a set of principles to live by. But where do you learn these values? My guiding principles can absolutely be traced back to my beloved mother, Bernarda (Rubia) Samuel Juliana. She is certainly the reason a passion for justice runs through my veins. In this chapter, I will share the fundamental principles my mom taught me so you can adopt some of them and/or develop your own.

My very first childhood memories are of my mother taking my cousin and me to a kindergarten somewhere in Otrabanda, a district in the capital city of Willemstad, Curaçao. Every morning before school, she would make a speech, *"Mi yu, korda hasi bo best na skol,"* which means, "My son, do the best you can at school and do it the right way."

Doing the best you can, doing the right thing—that was built into my mother's DNA. She never compromised her principles, and she taught her family and colleagues not to either. Her work environment, for example, always had to be clean, organized, and well-structured.

Fast forward a year, and after finishing kindergarten, it was time to go to primary school. My mother was born and raised in the neighborhood of Groot Kwartier, which had a couple of primary schools: St. Paul's College, Berg Carmel College, and Pablo Duarte College. Berg Carmel College was by far one of the best primary schools not only for the Groot Kwartier area but also for the whole island. The results and the number of children qualifying for high school were excellent. Only one small detail: Children from the Groot Kwartier area were not allowed to attend Berg Carmel College. The school was reserved for children from wealthy families and children who were not the descendants of black parents.

Clear signs of discrimination surrounded me—it wasn't only the primary school. Eight years before, on May 30, 1969, Curaçao was shocked by the first massive social disturbance, sparked by unequal pay for workers at the refinery. These workers marched to the capital, Willemstad, and the city was burned to ashes. So now there was this school, Berg Carmel College, located in an ordinary neighborhood, where not a single black child attended, nor any from the surrounding neighborhoods. The only children who attended Berg Carmel College were white and from wealthy families on the island.

Together with other parents, my mother formed a group that decided this was not acceptable—it was discrimination. They wrote letters to the Chief Deputy and Minister of Education of the Government of Curaçao to draw attention to the issue. It had been going on for many years at Berg Carmel College and was a common practice until 1977, when I, my niece, and ten other children from the neighborhood attended primary school. After many letters and peaceful demonstrations at the school's gate, we were accepted as the first black children at Berg Carmel College, a group of twelve children.

My mother had told me the reason they gave for not admitting black children to Berg Carmel College was that the school's annual graduation rate was excellent. The principal told my mother that admitting black children could affect the school's performance, which was a great threat to Berg Carmel College. My mother just told the other children to do their best to show the principal that their argument was nonsense. That was the first time I saw my mother's fighting spirit against injustice and inequality.

There would be many more lessons to come. It was from my mom, for example, that I would soon learn about the importance of honesty.

TELL THE TRUTH

When I was twelve years old and in the second year of high school, we had a teacher who was a tyrant. She could not explain the lessons' content and punished everyone who complained. Several complaints were filed against her, but no action was taken. So I decided to protect my classmates from this tyranny and placed a spoiled duck egg behind a closet in the classroom, which emitted a horrible smell. My father had a small farm of chickens and ducks, so one morning I collected a spoiled egg and carted it to school. The stench in the classroom made it impossible to teach or learn. When the teacher discovered the egg behind the closet, she was angry. She had thought it was a stink bomb. She threatened the entire class if the one responsible for this action did not identify himself. That's when I stood up and told her I was the one responsible, and that I did it because no one liked the way she was teaching. She sent me immediately to the vice principal's office.

In the vice principal's office, when I told her what happened, she could not believe I did something like that, because I was a model high school student. When I told her the reason, she said, "Gilbert, you could have asked for my attention regarding the misbehavior of the teacher. I will take care of it. But you must understand that I have to punish you for cleaning the classrooms in the afternoons. Additionally, I will write a letter that must be signed by your parents so they will be aware of what has happened."

My mind raced about how I would explain this to my mother and my father. I couldn't find a way, so I asked our favorite aunt, Maria Julia (Aunt Aya), to sign the letter, and she did. So, case closed, I thought. I told my mother I had to stay at school to help other students with mathematics, which is something I used to do. What I forgot was that my mother had a huge social network and she knew many people. One week after my punishment, she came home and asked me if I had something to tell her. I could sense from her intonation that she was not happy with something I had done.

"What exactly do you mean, Mom?" I said, trying to avoid a wrong answer.

"I am talking about how last week you stayed late at school to help some students with mathematics," she said.

I knew immediately she knew the truth, and I had to tell her. So I explained the egg incident and why I did not tell her.

"Listen, my son, I'm going to teach you a lesson that will be valuable for the rest of your life," she said, "and this is something you must teach your own children. *No gaña mi. Ta si bo bisa mi e bèrdat so mi por yuda bo.* Do not lie to me. I can help you only if you tell me the truth. No matter what the circumstances are, my son, always tell me the truth, because that's the only way I can help you when shit happens. You have to promise me you will never lie to me again."

I promised her I would never lie to her again, and I didn't.

GIVE TOUGH LOVE

Then, once during my first year of high school, I wanted to attend a birthday party. The party was for the son of a wealthy family, and my mother was very much against it, saying that the rich boy was spoiled. It was her firm opinion that a spoiled child lacks discipline and a sense of responsibility. She knew the family and knew how they raised their children, which was the opposite of how she raised us. For every pair of sneakers, bike, or fashion trend in the market, the children could ask their parents, and they would get it. Mom told me she would not give me permission to attend that party, and I explained that I must go because everyone at school was going.

"You are not everyone, and you are not going, period," she said, which made me cry. "*Mihó bo yora ku ami yora. Si ami tin ku yora, e doló ta mas grandi,"* she said, which means, "Better you cry now because I corrected you, than for me to cry later because I lost you."

My crying didn't change her mind.

While I was writing this book, my wife, Chantal, and I had to explain to our third son, Antoine, why we would not buy a scooter for him. In Curaçao, it is common for high school students to have their own scooters to get to school. Antoine wanted a scooter. We explained why it would not happen. As CEO of the general hospital of Curaçao, I shared with him the number of scooter accidents involving children that were brought to our emergency room. The number increased from six scooter accidents in 2019 to fifty in 2024, an increase of 833 percent, which is a point of great concern for the island of Curaçao. I told him what I had been told at his age: *"Mihó bo yora ku ami yora. Si ami tin ku yora, e doló ta mas grandi."*

BE BRAVE

Mom was not afraid of dying. From the time we were young, she prepared us that her passing away would not mean that she was gone. Her physical body would be gone, but she would be with us in spirit forever. Her expression, *"Dia mi ta muri, mi mes ta bisa boso,"* which means, "The day I will die, I will inform you," was one she spoke frequently. In her own way, she was preparing us not to be afraid of death.

When she called me on that day in August, she knew she was going to die. She called me and asked me to summon my brother and sister. *"Juny, mama a yama bo pa bo yama Pong i Gichi, pa bos nan bini serka, mama awe tardi,"* which translates as, "Juny, Mommy called you so you can call Pong and Gichi—I want all of you to come see me this afternoon." (My nickname was Juny, because my father's name was also Gilbert. Gilbert Junior became Juny in our local language, Papiamentu.)

When I called my brother and my sister, Gilian agreed to visit Mama immediately, but George hesitated. He explained he had had a long day at the office, and he would visit Mama tomorrow. But when

I arrived at the hospice center, and shortly after that, my sister, my mother said, *"Unda Pong a keda"*, which translates as, "Why am I not seeing Pong?" When I explained, she said, *"Yama Pong awor aki anto bis'é ku mama a manda bis'é pa e bini awor aki,"* which means, "Call Pong now and tell him that mommy said to come right now."

Mama always had a very specific look in her eyes when she demanded something. When we were young and she gave us this look, we knew it was over and out, no more arguing. As soon as George (Pong) arrived at the hospice center, she told us she was ready to go and meet her mother and brothers who had passed before us. *"Mama ta kla bai serka Oma, tio Sjors i tio Toontje pero mama no ke bai laga bosonan,"* which translates as, "Mommy is ready to go be with Grandma, uncle Sjors, and uncle Toontje, but mommy does not want to leave you all." We exchanged glances. We all understood she was asking our permission to leave this physical world, and we gave her that assurance. *"Mama, danki pa tur lokual mama a hasi pa nos, danki pa mama su amor, sabiduria i disiplina, nos ta priminti mama ku nos lo keda stima otro i kuida otro i tambe mama su ñetunan, ami lo hasi esaki,"* which means, "Mommy, thank you for everything you have done for us. Thank you for your love, wisdom, and discipline. We promise we will continue to love each other, take care of each other, and also take care of your grandchildren. This I promise you. I will do this!"

This gave her immediate relief. Shortly after that, she died. Mama had kept her word.

KNOW YOUR FRIENDS

Another guiding principle I learned from my mother was about the importance of friendship. But also to beware of what, in modern parlance, we would call "frenemies." Mom knew many people through her work, but she was extremely selective about who could visit her at home, and she taught us to be like that too. She always taught us to be aware of this from a young age. *"Djente blanku no ta kurason,"* which means, "White teeth do not represent the heart." She was educating us constantly to be aware of the ones who are really your friends and family, that it was not based on what you have, what you are, or what you have become, but it's based on their love and appreciation for you. People can be opportunistic, she told us, and they will pretend to be your friend because they need you for something, or because they want something from you. She reminded us that deep down in their hearts, they could be jealous, or they could hate you because they do not have what you have. Jealousy and envy are the opposite of what you must bring into your life. Instead, you must surround yourself with people who really love you and just forget about anyone else.

When my mother passed away in August 2023, she was surrounded by friends. We cherished the idea of how we could commemorate her during the funeral, expressing our unconditional love for her, her unconditional love for us, and what she meant to us. We decided to make a photo collage for the day of the funeral, showing all the sayings and pictures that corresponded with those sayings.

As background music, we chose the song "Goodness of God" by Cece Winans, an American Gospel singer, to express our gratitude for being blessed with such a wonderful mother and grandmother.

The collage of her favorite sayings was lovely and well received by everyone at the funeral. In fact, to this day, I often use many of these sayings in my life as a father, husband, and professional.

If you would like to incorporate some of my mother's favorite Papiamentu sayings into your life, you can find them in Figure 1.

PAPIAMENTU	ENGLISH	WISDOM
Dia mi ta muri, mi mes ta bisa boso	When I'm ready to go, I'll tell you myself.	Awareness
Warda bo awanan di wowo pa dia mi muri	Save your tears for the day I die.	Be strong
Ku muri, ta dera	Death comes, burial follows.	Life is relative
Ami por kue mi tas bai ki ora ku mi ke pasó mi ta haña trabou tur kaminda	I can pick up my bag and leave anytime—I'll find work anywhere.	Quality work gives you the right to stand your ground—always and everywhere.
Si bo hasi un kos, hasié na drechi	If you're going to do something, do it properly.	Excellence
Yama bo superior pa mi	Let me speak to your supervisor.	The power of escalation Determination Perseverance
Ta un Dios bo por sirbi	You can't walk two roads. You can't serve two masters. (Matthew 6:24)	Focus
Biba ku realidat	Live grounded in reality.	Be aware of your limitations
Para ku bo dos pianan riba tera	Live with both feet on the ground.	Always remain humble
Paña, kos, ni posishon no ta hasi bo hende	Clothes, possessions, and positions don't define who you are.	Self-discovery Authenticity True identity
Duna mi ora, ami ta traha ku ora	Tell me the time—I work with time.	Punctuality
No laga pa hende tin nada di bisa bo	Don't give people a reason to talk about you. Keep your name clean.	Reputation
Sòru pa bo no dependé di niun hende	Do not depend on anyone.	Self-reliance

PAPIAMENTU	ENGLISH	WISDOM
Siña konosé bo kurpa	Get to know your body.	Self-awareness Body awareness Auto-triage
Hende ta pidi ordensia!	Order, please!	Discipline Boundaries
Mi si ta mi si, mi nò ta mi nò	When I say yes, it's yes. When I say no, it's no.	Integrity Decisiveness
B'a bira gordu yu, *buska bahamentu*	You've gained a lot of weight—time to do something about that.	Healthy lifestyle
Dia mi muri mi ta sosegá	I'll rest when I die.	Work will not kill you
Buska siñamentu!	Put school first!	Don't get distracted
No gaña mi. Ta si bo bisa mi *bèrdat so mi por yuda bo*	Don't lie to me. I can only help you if you tell me the truth.	Honesty Accountability Trust Emotional safety
Promé bo bai hunga pafó, *sòru di hasi bo huiswerk*	Before you go play outside, make sure you've done your homework.	Priorities
Mi ta bon pa tir'afó, pero *no laga mi rabia*	I'm sweet, yes, but don't test my temper.	Boundaries
Mihó bo yora ku ami *yora. Si ami tin ku yora,* *e doló ta mas grandi*	Better you cry now because I corrected you, than I cry later because I lost you.	Tough love
Bida tin ku sigui	Life goes on.	Acceptance and resilience
Djente blanku no *ta kurason*	White teeth do not represent the heart.	Know who is your friend and who is your enemy

Figure 1: My mother's favorite sayings

CHAPTER 2

Our Brain, Our Mind, and Our Consciousness

Why is it so important to watch our thoughts? From where do our thoughts originate? Does an unhealthy mind generate unhealthy thoughts? In turn, does a healthy mind generate healthy thoughts?

I can remember my brother coming home after school and scooping up food. He would ask my mother, *"Mama kuantu kuminda mi tin mag di kue?"* which means, "Mother, how much food can I take?" My mother always answered, *"Mi yu, kue segun bo konsenshi, korda cu tin mas hende ta biba den kas i ku tin hende ku no ta haña di nada di kome,"* which means, "My son, take as much as your consciousness allows you to take. Remember that you are not the only one living in this house and there are people living in this world without a decent meal every day." My mother taught my brother to be gracious, not to be selfish, to show empathy, and to remember the children who don't get a decent meal every day.

Can an unhealthy mind create diseases? The answer to this last question is yes. Psychosomatic complaints and diseases involve physical symptoms that are influenced, triggered, or exacerbated by psychological factors, such as stress, anxiety, or depression. While the symptoms are real and often cause significant distress, there is no identifiable organic or structural cause for the condition. Instead, emotional and mental states are thought to play a key role. Extensive scientific research has explored the relationship between the mind and body in this context, aiming to understand the mechanisms underlying psychosomatic illnesses and to develop effective treatment strategies.

On the other hand, can a healthy mind create wellness? The answer to this question is also yes. Psychosomatic health refers to the intricate connection between the mind (psyche) and body (soma), and to the study of how psychological processes influence physical health and illness. The field of psychosomatic medicine explores how emotional, psychological, social, and behavioral factors interact with biological systems to influence the development and progression of disease. While psychosomatic disorders focus on specific conditions with prominent mind-body interactions, psychosomatic health encompasses the broader understanding of how mental states, stress, and emotions contribute to overall well-being and physical functioning.

The idea that mental and emotional states affect physical health is ancient. In Greek medicine, Hippocrates and Galen emphasized the balance of body and mind, and similar ideas are found in Eastern medical systems, such as Traditional Chinese Medicine, Ayurveda, Shamanism, and other ancient healing techniques described in the next chapter. Modern psychosomatic medicine gained momentum in the early twentieth century with psychoanalysis, in which Dr. Sigmund Freud and others posited that unconscious psychological conflicts could manifest as physical symptoms (e.g., conversion disorder). The integration of psychological, social, and biological aspects of health is best captured by the biopsychosocial model introduced by George Engel in 1977. This model is now a cornerstone of understanding psychosomatic health, as it emphasizes the complex interplay of biological, psychological, and social factors in health and illness.

UNDERSTANDING THE BRAIN AND MIND

Before we dive in, let's take a moment to understand the difference between the brain and mind. This distinction is crucial and can be a real eye-opener. The brain is not the mind. Most people think the brain and mind are the same, but they aren't. They are separate, yet inseparable. Your brain is a highly responsive physical organ made up of neurons and supporting tissues, all intricately connected to process and transmit information, regulate bodily functions, and enable complex behaviors and cognitive abilities. Its core function is to help you survive and thrive.

The mind is a process that emerges from the flow of information and energy within your brain/body and between you and your environment. Its core function is to monitor and regulate your conscious experience. You can think of the mind as the piano player and the brain as the piano. The music that arises from the piano is determined by how tuned the piano (functioning, health, and activity of the brain) is and how well it is played (the skill with which you use your mind). This is one of the key aspects of meditation, which will be described extensively in a chapter ahead.

Meditation is a collection of training methods that teach you how to use your mind to change your brain. Changes in our brains occur during neuroplasticity. Neuroplasticity is the brain's ability to reorganize itself by forming new neural connections throughout life. This allows the brain to adapt to experiences, learn new skills, recover from injuries, and compensate for lost functions. It occurs at different levels, from cellular changes in individual neurons to large-scale cortical remapping.

This, in turn, transforms your conscious experience, including your feelings, decisions, behaviors—everything. Meditation, especially when supported by neurofeedback, enables you to create the music you desire by becoming a proficient player of the piano—your brain. The more skilled you become, the greater your capacity to create the life experience you want. When your life and life experience are not what you want, you can change the music by using your mind to change your brain. This is what meditation teaches us. Change the way you think, change your thoughts, and you will change the way you perceive life and create a different destiny for your life.

OUR BRAIN

All human brains consist of four brains, which are:

- **The reptilian brain.** It is the oldest part of all four brains, and we share it with reptiles. It's responsible for all the autonomic functions of the body, from blood pressure to breathing.
- **The mammalian or limbic brain.** We share this brain with all other mammals. It is the principal center of our emotions and four fundamental programs—fear, food, fight, and reproduction. This is the brain that's unable to forgive. It functions from defensiveness and a sense of scarcity. The main structures of the limbic brain are the hippocampus, the amygdala, and the hypothalamus.
- **The neocortex brain.** Above the limbic brain is the neocortex, which is the brain of science, creativity, and mathematics. It's the brain the shamans sought to awaken if they wanted to create psychosomatic health. It comes to life when we nourish it with healthy fats, including olive oil, coconut oil, and avocado.
- **The "God Brain," or prefrontal cortex.** This is the only region of the brain that remains active at the peak of illumination and transcendence.

In their book *Power Up Your Brain: The Neuroscience of Enlightenment,* Dr. David Perlmutter and Dr. Alberto Villoldo describe the anatomy of our brains and our powerful mind (the healthy mind, if you will). They discuss how stress harms the brain, how we can prime our brains for enlightenment, and how we can power them up. Perlmutter is a neurologist and brain health expert, and Villoldo is a shaman and psychologist with expertise in Indigenous healing practices. The book attempts to merge two traditionally distinct approaches to human potential: modern neuroscience and ancient spiritual traditions. Through this synthesis, the authors offer readers a guide to optimize brain function and cultivate a state of enlightenment—a condition they describe as higher consciousness, balance, and harmony.

As an example of the content in their book, I'll briefly describe the three main sections: the scientific foundation, the spiritual tradition, and practical applications. This structure reflects the authors' collaborative effort to blend cutting-edge science with shamanic wisdom.

THE NEUROSCIENTIFIC PERSPECTIVE (PERLMUTTER)

Perlmutter, known for his work on brain health and neuroplasticity, argues that optimal brain function is essential for achieving spiritual enlightenment. He explains how chronic stress, toxins, poor nutrition, and inflammation can negatively affect brain function. These, in turn, block the attainment of a state of enlightenment or transcendence.

One key focus of the book is neurogenesis, the process of growing new neurons, which Perlmutter ties to achieving enlightenment. He advocates for nutritional interventions, particularly the inclusion of certain foods (like omega-3 fatty acids and antioxidants) and supplements (such as DHA, curcumin, and resveratrol) that support brain health. Perlmutter also introduces readers to the importance of balancing neurotransmitters like serotonin and dopamine, arguing that this balance is critical to maintaining mental clarity, emotional stability, and overall well-being.

THE SPIRITUAL AND SHAMANIC TRADITION (VILLOLDO)

Villoldo, drawing on his background in shamanic healing, presents the spiritual aspect by introducing the concept of luminous energy fields, which surround all humans and can be cleansed or strengthened to support healing. He discusses how ancient practices—such as meditation, breathwork, and rituals—can help align the body and mind, facilitating a state of enlightenment.

Villoldo explains that healing these energy fields is integral to removing obstacles to enlightenment. He provides a framework for understanding how trauma, negative emotions, and past-life experiences can block energy and lead to illness. His teachings align with modern ideas in psychosomatic medicine, suggesting that emotional and psychological healing are essential components of brain health. The spiritual aspect is not just metaphysical. Villoldo also weaves in the idea of epigenetics, the study of how lifestyle factors can influence gene expression. He posits that ancient practices help turn on genes that enhance brain function and turn off those that promote inflammation and illness. This fusion of spirituality with a scientific mechanism, such as epigenetics, is one of the book's unique selling points.

PRACTICAL APPLICATIONS

The book's final section offers practical strategies to enhance brain health and spiritual well-being. I'll include highlights here because they have helped me.

- **Dietary recommendations.** A specific nutritional plan designed to reduce inflammation and oxidative stress, thereby boosting brain power. The diet is rich in brain-healthy fats, lean proteins, and antioxidant-rich fruits and vegetables.
- **Meditation techniques.** Villoldo and Perlmutter offer various meditation practices to reduce stress and promote neuroplasticity. These techniques encourage a deep connection between the body, mind, and spirit.
- **Supplement protocols.** The authors recommend a range of supplements to support brain health, including omega-3 fatty acids, probiotics, and specific vitamins and minerals.
- **Detoxification practices.** This includes both physical detox (through diet and supplements) and emotional detox (through meditation and energy work) to cleanse the body and mind of toxic influences.

I emerged from this book with fascinating key themes and take-aways that I could take forward in my life, including:

- **Neuroplasticity and Enlightenment.** One key idea is that the brain is not fixed—it can be rewired and improved through lifestyle changes. This concept of neuroplasticity underpins many of the strategies in the book, from dietary choices to spiritual practices, as a way to enhance one's potential for enlightenment.
- **Holistic Brain Health.** The book stresses that achieving optimal brain health requires a holistic approach that includes diet, supplements, emotional healing, detoxification, and spiritual practices. Rather than viewing the brain and body as separate entities, the authors argue that brain function is deeply intertwined with physical health, emotional states, and spiritual well-being.
- **The Confluence of Science and Spirituality.** *Power Up Your Brain* is a bold attempt to bring together two worlds—modern neuroscience and ancient spiritual wisdom. Perlmutter provides a scientific foundation for many spiritual practices by referencing studies on neurotransmitters, neurogenesis, and epigenetics. Villoldo, meanwhile, grounds ancient practices in a scientific context, arguing that spirituality can influence genetic expression and neurochemistry.
- **Personal Empowerment and Healing.** The book encourages readers to take control of their brain health and spiritual well-being through accessible lifestyle changes. The overarching message is one of personal empowerment: You can rewire your brain and heal past traumas to achieve a higher state of consciousness and improve your quality of life.
- **Energy Medicine Meets Science.** Villoldo's teachings about the energy body, trauma, and emotional health intersect with Perlmutter's discussion on stress and inflammation. Both emphasize that unresolved emotional issues, whether through energy blockages or psychological distress, can prevent neuroplasticity and brain optimization.

This book was a revelation and game-changer for me when I read it in 2016/2017 before my first retreat to the Sanctuary Los Lobos of Alberto Villoldo and Marcela Lobos for the retreat "Grow a New Body," which is described in more detail in an upcoming chapter. On the first day of the retreat, Villoldo informed me, after scanning my luminous energy field, that I had an imprint on my heart chakra related to my relationship with my father. It was time to clear this imprint and start the healing process. This helped me build up my relationship with my father after more than thirty years, during which time the thoughts and emotions had become a wall of judgment, disappointment, isolation, and denial. This was costing me: it had manifested in my body.

So why is it so important to watch our thoughts? Because our thoughts can determine our destiny.

From where do our thoughts originate? There is no single answer, but our thoughts are shaped by many factors, including biological brain processes, psychological development, philosophical ideas about consciousness, and even cultural and spiritual influences. While neuroscience offers compelling explanations grounded in brain function and neurochemistry, philosophical and spiritual perspectives raise deeper questions about the nature of consciousness and the mind. Thought is a multifaceted phenomenon, emerging from the interplay among biology, experience, environment, and possibly even larger universal forces.

Does an unhealthy mind—a mind that has been shaped by traumas or other stress-inducing factors generate unhealthy thoughts? The answer is yes—that's what post-traumatic stress disorder is all about. This disorder develops in people who have experienced a shocking, scary, or dangerous event. It is natural to feel afraid during and after a traumatic situation. Fear is part of the body's fight-or-flight response, which helps us avoid or respond to potential danger.

Does a healthy mind generate healthy thoughts? The answer is yes! A healthy mind generates healthy thoughts, which lead to healthy human beings and healthy nations.

CHAPTER 3

Ego vs. True Self

We know that psychopathy is a disease; however, it is not recognized easily because psychopaths come across as normal individuals. The battle between ego and true self was first described by the renowned psychiatrist and psychoanalyst, Carl Jung. In this chapter, we'll turn to his writings to understand the pathology of the thinking and how it affects organizations and nations.

In *The Undiscovered Self: The Dilemma of the Individual of Modern Society*, Swiss psychoanalyst, Carl G. Jung sums up the conflict between the healthy and unhealthy mind when he describes the fight between ego and the True Self, writing, "The individual who is not anchored in God can offer no resistance on his own resources to the physical and moral blandishments of the world."

KEY CONCEPTS IN JUNGIAN PSYCHOLOGY

1. **The Collective Unconscious.** One of Jung's most important and original ideas is the notion of the collective unconscious, a part of the unconscious mind shared by all humans due to common evolutionary history. Unlike Freud's personal unconscious (formed

from individual experiences), the collective unconscious contains universal archetypes and inherited patterns of behavior. It's responsible for certain myths, symbols, and instinctual behaviors found across all human cultures.

2. **Archetypes.** Jung introduced the concept of archetypes as universal, primal symbols, or motifs recurring across cultures, art, literature, and religion. These archetypes emerge from the collective unconscious. Some of the most important archetypes include:

    A. **The Self.** Represents the unified psyche as a whole, and the goal of psychological development (individuation) is to integrate various aspects of the self.

    B. **The Shadow.** Represents the dark, repressed, and unknown aspects of one's personality, often projected onto others.

    C. **The Anima and Animus.** Represents the unconscious feminine side in men (anima) and the unconscious masculine side in women (animus). They are crucial for understanding gender, attraction, and relationships in Jungian psychology.

    D. **The Persona.** Represents the "mask" or façade that individuals present to the world, often shaped by societal expectations.

Individuation is the process of integrating the conscious and unconscious aspects of the personality to achieve wholeness and self-realization. According to Jung, individuation is the central goal of human life and psychological development, allowing individuals to realize their full potential. It involves confronting and integrating the shadow, balancing the anima/animus, and reconciling various conflicting aspects of the personality.

Synchronicity is another key concept in Jung's work, which refers to meaningful coincidences that are not causally related but have significant meaning to the person experiencing them. Jung argued that such events reveal an underlying connection between the individual and the larger cosmos, reflecting a deeper order beyond the realm of traditional cause-and-effect. Synchronicity is what the shamans call *agni,* which means reciprocity and living in balance and harmony with all living beings and the cosmos. It rests on the belief that the cosmos co-creates with the individual. It looks like magic because the intentions of the individual are the same as the cosmos, and this creates beauty and abundance for a general purpose.

Like Freud, Jung viewed dreams as windows into the unconscious. However, rather than seeing dreams as expressions of repressed desires, Jung believed they represented unconscious attempts at communication with the conscious mind. He saw dreams as a way for the unconscious to provide insight into unresolved issues and the process of individuation. Jung's approach to dreams often involved interpreting symbols, archetypes, and myths. Jung was deeply interested in religion, mythology, and alchemy, which he studied as representations of the human psyche. His research led him to explore various world religions and spiritual practices, including Christianity, Hinduism, Buddhism, and Indigenous spiritual traditions. Jung believed religious symbols and myths express fundamental psychological truths and that spirituality could be a path toward psychological healing.

His study of alchemy, which began in the 1920s, was particularly significant. Jung saw alchemy as a symbolic process of transformation, reflecting the process of individuation. He interpreted alchemical symbols as representations of psychological processes, with the philosopher's stone symbolizing the integration of the self. His 1944 book, *Psychology and Alchemy,* is one of his major works on the subject.

The concepts of the ego and the soul represent two distinct aspects of human existence, often framed within psychology, philosophy, and spiritual traditions. While both are central to our understanding of identity, consciousness, and being, they are fundamentally different in their nature, purpose, and influence on our lives.

Ego refers to the aspect of the self associated with individual identity, personal perspective, and the sense of self that interacts with the world. Ego is concerned with survival, self-preservation, and social functioning. The ego defines itself in relation to external experiences, people, and circumstances. Rooted in rationality, the ego operates in the realm of the mind and thought. It is the construct through which we develop a sense of "I," or who we are in relation to our thoughts, emotions, and external stimuli. As described in the previous chapter, it is important to watch our thoughts, as they can shape our destiny. A healthy mind is key to developing nourishing thoughts.

According to psychoanalytic theory developed by Freud and Jung, the ego develops as part of the conscious mind and serves as the mediator between our primitive desires (the Id, in Freud's terminology) and moral considerations (the superego, also from Freud). The ego forms in early childhood as we differentiate ourselves from others, build self-awareness, and learn societal rules. The ego helps us navigate the world, providing a framework for interacting with reality. It helps us make decisions, set goals, and protect ourselves from harm. It is responsible for self-image and self-esteem. The ego can be fragile when its identity is challenged, leading to defensive reactions or efforts to control external outcomes. The ego focuses on comparisons and external validation. It is often concerned with how others perceive us, our status, material possessions, and power. These are mainly functions of the mammalian or limbic brain, as described in a previous chapter. The ego operates largely through fear, insecurity, and attachment to external realities. Because it seeks validation from external circumstances, it is highly reactive, defensive, and easily threatened. It often leads to the creation of a false self or an illusory sense of identity that can be dominated by pride, arrogance, or self-centeredness. This can make it difficult to experience deeper, more authentic connections with others and oneself. The ego associates with duality and separation—separating the self from others and from the larger fabric of existence.

The soul represents the essence of the individual—a deeper, eternal, and universal aspect of being. It is often considered the True Self, transcending physical form, the mind, and the ego. While the ego is time-bound and shaped by societal and personal experiences, the soul is viewed as timeless, connected to the divine, or the broader spiritual realm. The soul is associated with inner wisdom, intuition, love, compassion, and a sense of oneness with the universe. It operates from a place of peace, connectedness, and spiritual purpose.

In many spiritual traditions, such as Hinduism, Christianity, or Sufism, the soul is seen as the eternal part of a person, connected to the divine source or God. It is the aspect of the self that seeks truth, enlightenment, and union with a higher power. Philosophers like Plato described the soul as the immortal essence of a person, distinct from the body and mind. It is often viewed as the seat of true wisdom and moral understanding. In contrast to the ego's focus on separateness, the soul embodies the unity of all things, transcending individual identity. The soul guides us toward our higher purpose and spiritual growth. It is the source of deep joy, meaning, and a sense of connection to all life. It operates at the levels of intuition, feeling, and inner knowing, often in contrast to the ego's rational, calculative nature. The soul expresses itself through qualities like empathy, creativity, and compassion, leading to actions that reflect a sense of service and unity with others.

The soul motivates us to act from a place of authenticity, driven by love, truth, and a desire for greater harmony with the universe. In contrast, the ego's motivations often stem from fear, a need for control, and self-protection. The soul's desires are generally not driven by external rewards or social validation, while the ego craves recognition, success, and approval from others.

Many spiritual practices quiet or transcend the ego, allowing the soul's wisdom to emerge. This can happen through meditation, mindfulness, prayer, or other means of self-exploration and spiritual connection. This is what will be described in Part IV: Ancestral Healing Wisdom. The ego creates illusions and attachments that prevent us from experiencing our true self, the soul. Transcending the ego involves letting go of these attachments and recognizing the impermanent nature of external identities and desires.

The ego and the soul often appear to be in conflict, as the ego is concerned with external realities, survival, and individual identity, while the soul is focused on internal truth, connection, and a higher purpose. This conflict manifests as inner turmoil (mental and physical diseases), where one feels torn between pursuing material success or external validation (ego-driven desires) and following a path of inner peace, spiritual growth, and purpose (soul-driven desires). The ego may resist the soul's guidance because it fears the loss of control or security, while the soul moves beyond the limitations imposed by the ego.

Some psychological and spiritual traditions suggest that rather than seeing the ego and soul as enemies, they should be seen as parts of a whole that can be integrated. The ego, when balanced, can serve a functional role in helping us navigate everyday life without overshadowing the soul's deeper wisdom. Integration involves becoming aware of the ego's tendencies and aligning its desires with the soul's deeper purpose. This process of aligning the ego with the soul is often seen as the path to self-actualization or spiritual awakening. It's our wake-up call from the dream that we are living—we are not our clothes, our cars, our houses. We are not our titles, our jobs, or our money in the bank account. We are much more than all those temporary, external, and relative mundane possessions. It's like the trilogy movie of *The Matrix,* where the main character, Neo, is asked which pill he wants—blue or red. The blue pill leads to an awakening that the world he is living in is not the real world. The red pill keeps him in the surrealistic world he lives in, with all its earthbound traditions. The blue pill is the awakening, and the red pill is the ego.

The ego's role in self-discovery is often necessary in the early stages of personal development. It helps individuals differentiate themselves, develop confidence, and navigate the material world.

However, as one progresses on a spiritual journey, one often realizes that the ego's identity is only a small part of who we truly are. The quest for deeper meaning leads to the recognition of the soul as the core of existence. The soul's journey involves moving beyond egoic desires and attachments, seeking connection with the divine, and realizing the unity of all beings.

ASPECT	EGO	SOUL (TRUE SELF)
Nature	Temporal identity-based	Eternal essence of being
Focus	External (material world, social identity)	Internal (spiritual connection, truth)
Motivation	Fear, control, validation	Love, compassion, unity
Purpose	Survival, self-protection, and status	Spiritual growth, higher purpose
Sense of Self	Individuality, separation	Unity, oneness
Function	Mediates reality, maintains self-image	Guides inner wisdom, higher consciousness
Emotions	Pride, fear, defensiveness, insecurity	Peace, joy, empathy, compassion
Endurance	Finite, attached to the body and mind	Infinite, transcends physical life

Figure 2: Ego vs. true self

In his book *Ego Is the Enemy*, Ryan Holiday explores the role of ego as an obstacle to personal and professional growth, encouraging readers to recognize and manage it to lead a more meaningful and fulfilling life. He said, "Ego is the enemy of what you want and of what you have." Divided into three sections—Aspire, Success, and Failure—the book draws on the stories of historical and modern figures to illustrate how ego can derail ambition, cloud judgment, and prevent genuine accomplishment. I turned to Holiday's book because I was fascinated by the simple yet powerful way the title illustrates that our ego is our biggest enemy to achieving a healthy mind and healthy nations. The historical and modern figures described in this book clearly identify the success or failure of individuals as based on egocentric or true self-behavior. I have included the names of historical and modern nation leaders who led their countries through egocentric or true self-leadership, and the results, which illustrate the importance of healthy minds. It confirms the title of my book: *Healthy Minds, Healthy Nation*. Unhealthy minds create unhealthy nations, and healthy minds create healthy nations.

Holiday describes ego as a person's unhealthy belief in their own importance, a desire for recognition, and a constant pursuit of validation. This ego can lead to self-centeredness, overconfidence, and ultimately poor decision-making. He argues that ego blinds individuals to their weaknesses and stunts their growth, often creating more problems than it solves.

Part I of the book (Aspire) discusses how ego is a threat in the initial stages of one's journey. Holiday emphasizes the importance of staying humble, embracing hard work, and learning from others rather than focusing solely on status or outward appearances. He draws lessons from the lives of people like Howard Hughes and Genghis Khan to show how those who let ego control them at the start often falter early. He advises individuals to focus on process and personal development, rather than seeking fame or titles.

In Part II (Success), Holiday describes how ego can be an especially deceptive enemy. Holiday argues that once people achieve some level of success, they often become complacent, believe their own hype, and lose the humility that helped them succeed. He discusses how National Football League coach Bill Belichick, for instance, maintained discipline and humility despite his many successes, making decisions based on strategy rather than his ego.

In Part III (Failure), Holiday suggests that ego makes failure more painful and enduring than it needs to be, as it encourages people to blame others, deny their mistakes, or become overly defensive. Figures like Katharine Graham serve as examples of individuals who overcame failure by remaining adaptable and open to learning, instead of letting their pride stand in the way. Katharine Graham was an American business executive who owned and published various news publications, most notably *The Washington Post*, which she transformed into one of the leading newspapers in the United States. Graham made her mark in history by publishing the Pentagon Papers, which showed the extent to which the government had misled the American people during the Vietnam War, and reporting on the Watergate break-in that eventually forced the resignation of President Richard Nixon.

This section of the book shows that failure, approached with humility, can be an invaluable learning tool and a stepping stone to later success.

THE KEY CONCEPTS AND PRINCIPLES OF *EGO IS THE ENEMY*

Embrace Humility. Instead of fixating on ambition or public recognition, Holiday suggests that genuine success comes from developing skills, contributing to a cause, and understanding one's weaknesses.

Continuous Learning and Improvement. Ego often inhibits learning by making people assume they know everything. Holiday advises readers to prioritize growth, stay curious, and remain open to feedback and criticism.

Self-Control and Discipline. The book emphasizes the importance of self-restraint and discipline to prevent ego from taking control. Rather than succumbing to praise, one should stay focused on goals and strive for lasting excellence.

The Value of Mentorship and Service. Holiday argues that one way to manage ego is through mentorship and service. By helping others, one stays grounded, learns valuable lessons, and finds a more sustainable source of fulfillment than ego-driven pursuits.

For me, the key takeaways of *Ego is the Enemy* are:

- Ego is a constant challenge, not a one-time battle. Recognizing and managing it requires continuous effort and vigilance.
- True success is about impact, not ego gratification. Holiday argues that one's achievements are more meaningful and enduring when they arise from genuine contributions rather than a desire for applause.
- Failure can be a gift. When approached with humility, failure teaches resilience and growth. The ego often distorts failure, but humility can make it a valuable lesson. Resist entitlement and embrace hard work. True fulfillment comes from disciplined effort and humility, rather than a sense of entitlement or desire for quick recognition.

I have experienced all of the above during my career, and the book helped me recognize the importance of being conscious and feeding my true self instead of my ego. Over time, our moral compass has been well developed so that no matter how great the temptation, or how great the failure, we will keep going on, guided by humility and service, seeking success measured by impact and not by ego gratification. During my fourteen-year career at ENNIA, there were huge temptations about money and power when I was offered more money to be less of a "troublemaker." During my period as chairman of the supervisory board at the refinery, failing to find a new operator for the refinery felt like a gift and a sign that it's time to let go, it's time for an energy transition for Curaçao, it's time for a Pachacutti. Last but not least, during my eight years of involvement with the new Curaçao Medical Center, it was important to resist entitlement as CEO of the new hospital of Curaçao and embrace hard work.

Ego Is the Enemy ultimately serves as a guide for navigating the modern pressures of ambition, success, and failure with humility and self-awareness. By learning to recognize and manage ego, readers can aspire to live a life defined by purpose, resilience, and meaningful achievement rather than empty recognition or fleeting success. I have experienced all of the above during my twenty-three-year career on my birth island, Curaçao, since I returned in 2003. It was an environment dominated by money, power, bribery, and huge egos. Sometimes I make the joke with close friends that if it were possible to extract, package, and sell ego as a product, Curaçao would be an extremely rich country with no debt.

Our journey in earthly life is to dissolve our ego before it dissolves our self, as Canadian hockey player Maxime Lagacé once stated. I have been in environments where the development of my true self was accelerated. I'm grateful for the opportunities and all the gifts the universe has given me, starting with the education and love from my parents, their divorce, which had a huge impact on me, my own journey as an unconsciously traumatized child, and last but not least, my awakening journey. In retrospect, I would never have wanted to miss these experiences. *Ego is the Enemy* helped me understand this extremely well.

THE HISTORY OF THE UNHEALTHY MIND

Throughout history, several nations or empires have collapsed or suffered severe decline due to the actions of egocentric leaders. These leaders often prioritized personal power, glory, or self-interest over the well-being of their country, leading to internal strife, economic collapse, or external invasions. Egocentric leaders can be characterized as having an unhealthy mindset. To understand the collective unhealthy mind, and how it has shaped human history, as well as our personal history, let me take you on a tour of the Caribbean, Central America, South America, North America, Europe, Africa, the Middle East, Asia, and the Pacific.

NAZI GERMANY UNDER ADOLF HITLER (1933–1945)—EUROPE

- Adolf Hitler, the leader of Nazi Germany, is one of the most notorious examples of a leader whose extreme egocentrism and ideological obsession led to the destruction of his country.

THE ZAIRE (DEMOCRATIC REPUBLIC OF CONGO) UNDER MOBUTU SESE SEKO (1965–1997)—AFRICA

- Mobutu Sese Seko ruled Zaire (now the Democratic Republic of Congo) with an authoritarian, kleptocratic regime marked by extreme corruption and self-aggrandizement.
- He used the country's wealth for personal enrichment, promoting a cult of personality in which his image and influence dominated all aspects of life.

THE CENTRAL AFRICAN EMPIRE UNDER EMPEROR BOKASSA (1966–1979)—AFRIKA

- Jean-Bédel Bokassa, who crowned himself Emperor of the Central African Empire (formerly the Central African Republic) in 1976, was notorious for his narcissistic and extravagant rule.
- He spent vast amounts of the nation's limited resources on his lavish coronation and personal luxuries, while his people lived in poverty.

HAITI UNDER FRANÇOIS "PAPA DOC" DUVALIER (1957–1971)—CARIBBEAN

- Duvalier ruled Haiti as a dictator with an egocentric and brutal approach.
- He fostered a cult of personality, portraying himself as a mystical, god-like figure, and used fear, propaganda, and the notorious Tonton Macoute secret police to maintain control.

IRAQ UNDER SADDAM HUSSEIN (1979–2003)—MIDDLE EAST

- Saddam Hussein, the authoritarian ruler of Iraq, led with an egocentric and ruthless hand.
- He engaged in numerous violent purges, promoted a cult of personality, and waged disastrous wars, such as the Iran–Iraq War (1980–1988) and the invasion of Kuwait in 1990, which led to the Gulf War.

NORTH KOREA UNDER KIM JONG-IL (1994–2011) AND KIM JONG-UN (2011–PRESENT)—ASIA

- Both Kim Jong-il and his son, Kim Jong-un, have ruled North Korea with an obsessive focus on maintaining their dynastic rule and personal power.

- The Kim family has fostered a cult of personality around themselves, demanding absolute loyalty and control over all aspects of life in North Korea.

THE PHILIPPINES UNDER FERDINAND MARCOS (1965–1986)—PACIFIC

- Ferdinand Marcos ruled the Philippines with an iron fist, imposing martial law in 1972 to extend his rule and suppress opposition.
- His leadership was characterized by widespread corruption, the enrichment of his family and close associates, and the suppression of civil liberties.

VENEZUELA UNDER NICOLÁS MADURO (2013–PRESENT)—SOUTH AMERICA

- Nicolás Maduro's leadership has been marked by a focus on maintaining personal power and the power of his political party, often at the expense of Venezuela's economy and democratic institutions.
- Despite widespread opposition and economic collapse, Maduro has continued to suppress dissent and manipulate elections.

In all these examples, the unhealthy mind prevailed—a mind primarily driven by thoughts based on an egocentric existence. The result was devastating for countries and humanity. These examples show us the importance of healthy minds as individuals, but more importantly as leaders of nations, because the impact is devastating if a nation is led by an egocentric leader.

Science clearly shows that the fight-or-flight mode is activated in our mammalian brains. We know from science and ancient healing therapies that we can heal our wounds. We can convert our wounds into gifts. Pain is inevitable, but suffering is a choice and not a punishment. True self-mastery applies to leaders who are deeply self-aware, guided by a sense of moral duty, and who prioritize collective well-being over personal power or gain. These leaders are typically characterized by humility, integrity, a vision for the future, and the ability to inspire their people toward positive change. The following are examples of nations led by true self-leaders.

INDIA UNDER MAHATMA GANDHI (MORAL LEADER, 1919–1948)—INDIA

- Mahatma Gandhi, though not an official head of state, was the moral and political leader of India's independence movement.
- His concept of satyagraha, nonviolent resistance, and commitment to truth, justice, and equality made him an embodiment of self-leadership.

SOUTH AFRICA UNDER NELSON MANDELA (1994–1999)—AFRICA

- Nelson Mandela's leadership of South Africa was marked by his selfless commitment to ending apartheid and promoting racial reconciliation.
- After spending twenty-seven years in prison for fighting against racial segregation, Mandela emerged with a vision of peace, unity, and forgiveness, placing the well-being of the nation above personal vengeance or gain.

NORWAY UNDER KING HAAKON VII (1905–1957)—EUROPE

King Haakon VII of Norway, who ruled after the country gained independence from Sweden in 1905, was widely respected for his humble, selfless leadership. Singapore Under Lee Kuan Yew (1959–1990)—Asia.

- Lee Kuan Yew, the first Prime Minister of Singapore, led with a focus on pragmatic governance, meritocracy, and long-term vision.

- Lee was known for his unwavering commitment to transforming Singapore from a struggling, resource-poor city-state into one of the world's most successful economies.

URUGUAY UNDER JOSÉ MUJICA (2010-2015)—SOUTH AMERICA

- José Mujica, known as the "world's humblest president," was famous for his modest lifestyle and selfless governance.
- A former guerrilla fighter turned president, Mujica lived in a simple farmhouse, donated most of his salary to charity, and avoided the trappings of power.

COSTA RICA UNDER ÓSCAR ARIAS (1986–1990, 2006-2010)—CENTRAL AMERICA

- Óscar Arias, a Nobel Peace Prize laureate, led Costa Rica with a focus on peace, democracy, and sustainable development.
- He is best known for his efforts to bring peace to Central America during the 1980s, particularly through his role in brokering the Esquipulas Peace Agreement.

UNITED STATES UNDER GEORGE WASHINGTON (1789-1797)—NORTH AMERICA

- George Washington, the first President of the United States, exemplified self-leadership through his refusal to seek absolute power and his dedication to establishing a democratic system.
- After leading the American colonies to victory in the Revolutionary War, Washington voluntarily relinquished military power, later setting a precedent by stepping down after two terms as president.

- Obama's presidency was marked by progressive policies, economic recovery, and significant social changes, though he also faced political opposition, particularly from a divided Congress.

In each of these examples, true self-leadership was characterized by humility, service to others, moral integrity, and a focus on the long-term well-being of the nation over personal ambition. These leaders inspired positive change by putting people's needs first, often in times of great challenge and transformation. Their legacies continue to serve as models for ethical, self-aware leadership. These were leaders with healthy minds who thought in terms of unity instead of individuality. It is important to realize that a human being who is capable of hurting another human being or any other living being is a human being in pain.

In Part IV, we will explore how meditation and ancient shamanic healing therapies can help every human being who is in pain due to traumas in this life or past lives. Traumas that are trapped in the psyche form an obstacle for tapping into the light within that connects us with every other living being, and the realization that hurting another living being comes from deep pain that we have healed.

CHAPTER 4

Embracing a Service Mindset

My mother worked as a physician's assistant, mainly for dermatologists. During my early years, she worked at a practice run by Dr. Den Ouden outside the hospital, but after a while, the dermatologists moved to work in the hospital, and my mother moved with them. We often visited her at St. Elizabeth Hospital. All the patients and colleagues loved my mother. She was organized and disciplined, and expected the same from everyone. Her patients loved her because she would always go the extra mile to help them. She was a walking library for patients, friends, and family—anyone who needed advice about their health went to my mother.

In her off time, after work or during the weekend, my mother was a local Mother Teresa, holding appointments with family and friends who needed health advice. My mother was known for providing prescription injections for patients who were dismissed from the hospital or who had a chronic illness that required daily injections. All those patients called her. She would drive to their homes and make sure the patients got their shots. She would also be called for advice about life in general: problems with children, problems in the neighborhood, or problems between a married couple.

As a child, I was a keen observer of all the ways my mom helped others. Her dedication to service rubbed off on me and was part of the inner foundation I built on when, much later in life, I sought transformation through transcendental meditation and shamanism.

As you pursue your path toward a healthier mind, for your individual benefit as well as that of your community/nation, I encourage you to embrace the service mentality exemplified by my mom. We can't all be Mother Teresa, but it's never too late to commit to helping others. In fact, it is a crucial ingredient for developing the sense of oneness, in contrast to an ego-driven identity, that awaits you on the other side of your journey.

Sharing is key. Life is not about hoarding or the endless accumulation of personal wealth and possessions.

SHARING IS CARING

In my grandmother's house, there had to be enough food for everyone. I remember on Friday afternoons, my grandmother instructed us to stand at the gate of the house and ask all the children who passed by after school if they wanted to drink water or eat some bread. This was her way of teaching us compassion and to be kind to everyone. She would tell us, "We must live with our neighbors, in order to die with God."

My other three aunts were nurses, and among my uncles, the oldest, George Juliana, was a biology teacher at Peter Stuyvesant College High School—the other three worked mostly in construction and had their own construction companies. I was not aware of the ancestral connection of my great-grandmother Gan to the Arawak, but during my transformative journey, I have become aware of her presence, strength, and wisdom.

Although I did not know Gan—she passed away long before I was born—I only saw pictures of her—I know she had a typical old Indian lady's small face, long chin, and two dark braids that cascaded to her hips. Gan was a landowner who lived in the neighborhood of Groot Kwartier, and she gave land to many families and friends. In a way, I'm convinced my passion to help humanity was inherited from Gan.

From the stories my mother told us about her, it seems that Gan was disciplined. Her way was the law that everyone should follow. I am convinced that my great-grandmother's lineage traces back to the Arawaks, the first inhabitants of the island of Curaçao, who came from South America, and my connection to shamanism. More about that later as we go along—I would need to have a life crisis to get more curious about that.

At my parents' house, we had many visitors, both from my mother's and my father's side, because they were both social and knew many people. During the weekends, the talk was always about the delicious meals my father had cooked. He was the expert in the kitchen and always paid a lot of attention to all the ingredients he used for his meals. I would go to the supermarket with him and learn from him why it was so important to choose the best of the best for every meal you cook. Everything should be fresh and handpicked to make sure the product has the best quality and taste. He would love to have visitors in the house so everyone could eat the meals he prepared. It was a beautiful and warm process to see how everyone enjoyed my father's meals. His passion for cooking was adorable, and that's where my passion for cooking comes from. I'm truly blessed to have spent my youth with both my father and my mother. My father instilled in me the passion for cooking, nature, and music. My mother instilled in me discipline, compassion, and empathy.

CHAPTER 5

Stories Give Us Hope

Elis Juliana was a well-known Curaçao poet, writer, visual artist, and archaeologist. Elis wrote poetry, short stories, and haikus. He represented Curaçao several times in international exhibitions with sculptures and paintings. Elis visited my grandmother a few times a week after work—the front or back porch was their favorite place to meet and talk. Every time Ompi Els, meaning Uncle Elis, visited my grandmother, we loved being there because before he left her house, he always told us a story. Ompi Els had so many stories! Among his favorite stories were the stories of *Kompa Nanzi*, or Comrade Nanzi. Nanzi was a spider named after the word *anansi* in the Akan language, the most widely spoken language of Ghana, from which most of the slaves shipped to Curaçao came. Kompa Nanzi is the Caribbean version of *Anansi*—the famous spider trickster from West African folklore.

Anansi stories certainly existed at the beginning of the intercontinental slave trade in the seventeenth century. Many stories about Kompa Nanzi were told to us during our childhood, sometimes in the afternoon or just before bedtime. The ones that made the most impact celebrated the cleverness of Kompa Nanzi, who came up with a solution even though in that dire moment it seemed like there was no hope. He found himself at the end of his life and the life of his family. In a certain sense, the saying "Every dark cloud has a silver lining" was the life philosophy that ran through the stories of Kompa Nanzi. I loved the stories because they told us to always be optimistic, no matter how hopeless the situation might be. Kompa Nanzi always maintained a healthy mind—a skill that served me well as I navigated adult life. Kompa Nanzi cultivated a positive mind with a solution for every challenge that we face in life—a mind that held hope and the vision of a better future.

Ompi Elis carried within him so many stories about Kompa Nanzi. Each time he told us a different story with so much passion and glamour that we felt like we were in a theater watching a performance by a professional storyteller, which he was. Popular stories about Kompa Nanzi included "Kompa Nansi and the Tar Doll" and "Kompa Nanzi and the Spotted Cow."

From these tales, I learned the power of storytelling. In particular, I saw how stories allow us to reframe seemingly hopeless situations, focusing on developing a healthy mind.

Remember, as you enjoy these stories, that Nanzi is a wise, cheerful, and mischievous spider who has adventures with his animal friends. He always gets something out of every situation, no matter how hopeless it might be.

Let me share a story my mother told us almost every morning when she took us to school, or in the afternoon when she picked us up. My mother was the oldest daughter of my grandmother; she had three sisters and four brothers. My grandmother raised her children alone. My mother decided before finishing primary school that she would quit school, and she helped my grandmother raise her brothers and sisters, because she didn't have the opportunity to finish high school.

From a young age, she made sure her children had the same opportunities she had. So, every time she drove us to school, she told us stories about the importance of the workforce within a community. Every human being is gifted in what he or she can do, and we have to respect that. Then she pointed out workers who were cleaning the streets, or workers who were digging along the road. She stressed the importance of the work they were doing. "We have to respect and honor every type of work, because it is necessary." Ask yourself what type of work you want to do in the future. Do you want to be a cleaner or a digger, or do you want another job? If you don't want to be a cleaner or a digger, make sure you do your best at school, and remember that every job and every person is important. It was her way of motivating us to be the best version of ourselves. A version that gives us hope, a version that would give us the opportunity to do good not only for ourselves but for every human being living around us. My mother had so many stories based on her fighting spirit for justice and equal opportunities.

I remember one day she told us the stories of how the medical director of the Saint Elizabeth Hospital in Curaçao told her she had to move to the basement with one of the dermatologists. The reason was that the working relationship with the other dermatologist was deteriorating, and it affected the patients. She explained to me how she requested a meeting with both the dermatologist and the medical director. She said she was not moving anywhere, and the issue was that they were not communicating because both of them thought they were better than the other.

"It's not a matter of being better. It's being at service for your patients, and both of you are doing a lousy job at this moment. So, you have a choice. You will work together and cooperate for the benefit of the patients, or I will quit as the head nurse of the department of dermatology."

Then it became still in the room. Everyone looked at each other with wide-open eyes. From that moment on, the cooperation between the two dermatologists became very close. Later, the medical director called her and told her she had solved an issue that had been a major challenge for the hospital's board. "It's your job, not mine, but if you don't do your job, I will do it for you."

My mother had so much courage and strength, and her stories

were an inspiration to me to be the best version of myself and to be hopeful about a bright future. My mother's first story and daily routine motivated me to do my best at school. I think deep inside she wanted to give us the chance she did not have to finish primary school. And the second story was how to deal with conflicts. That was a valuable lesson I'm still using today.

CHAPTER 6

What Does It Mean to Be a Peacemaker

How does being a peacemaker relate to developing a healthy mind and nation? Committing yourself to the identity of a peacemaker means seeking to understand before worrying about being understood. A peacemaker will always base their actions on the general interest instead of personal interest. Peacemakers think and live in terms of "We—Spirit—Oneness" and not in terms of "I—Ego—Individual."

In this chapter, we will look closely at what it means to be a peacemaker. If I had to summarize the main characteristics, I would say the following about peacemakers:

1. Peace rules in their heart.
2. Peacemakers are active, not passive.
3. Peacemakers are gentle.
4. Peacemakers are resolute in the truth.
5. Peacemakers are patient.

I learned the power of being a peacemaker in kindergarten. I witnessed my first impactful conflict and felt I had to step in and solve it. It's my first memory of a deep sense of pain and humiliation. On the playground at Kokolishi Kleuterschool, which is near the church of Groot Kwartier, I saw two boys holding down another boy. A third boy was throwing mango leaves on his head. This felt like humiliation too much to endure. This boy was being detained and restrained by the other two. He could not move. A rising urge to create peace from this situation welled up in me. I stepped forward and asked the three boys to kindly leave him alone.

"Stop throwing the leaves on his head," I said. "Why are you holding this boy? Why are you throwing leaves on his head?"

The one throwing the leaves responded, "During breaks, he talks and plays with a friend of mine, a girl." Turning to the boy, he said, "I do not like that idea of you talking and playing with this girl at all."

Then I asked him, "Why don't you want him to talk to her? Is she your sister or family? Do you own her?"

"She is not my sister, nor my family," he answered. "I simply do not want him to talk or play with her during the breaks."

Then I asked him, "Aren't we all supposed to come to school, learn, talk, and help each other? Can you imagine if you were the one the two other boys were holding down? Can you see the way you are humiliating him in front of everyone?"

Then I noticed he hadn't responded, and he looked like he was thinking deeply. The mirror I had used about coming to school to learn, talk, and help others was my mother talking. I had tapped into her wisdom to calm down a violent event. When I posed my questions, it apparently left him in deep shock.

He told the other two boys, "Leave him alone, and stop throwing the leaves on him."

Then I said to all of them, "We do not come to school to fight, humiliate, or bully each other. We come to school to learn, talk, and help each other. We are brothers and sisters, and brothers should care and help each other."

To all of them, I repeated that our purpose at school is to learn, help each other, and not hurt each other. I asked them to promise to stick to learning and helping each other. They agreed, and the scene of humiliation was over.

This moment was an action I did not have to think about—it happened instantaneously when I saw what was happening and could sense the pain and humiliation of the victimized boy.

"WE HAVE A LITTLE SISTER NOW"

I have a brother, George, who is four years younger and a younger sister, Gilian, who is nine years younger. George's wish was to have a little brother and not a little sister. Therefore, when he learned that a baby girl was on the way, not a baby boy, he was not happy at all. The first day my parents came home with our little newborn sister, she cried a lot. George asked my mother if she could not stick an apple in her mouth so he would not have to hear her crying.

"How could you ask Mama to do such a selfish thing?" I asked him. "It is not only about your peace of mind. We have a little sister now, and we have to take care of her too."

"Her crying is hurting my ears," he said.

"I can understand that you have to get used to the presence of our little sister, but you have to promise me you will help me, mother, and father take care of her," I said.

"I promise," he said.

Over the years, it took many talks with George to encourage him to love Gilian as his little sister. The way I see it now is that he was jealous because Gilian was the first granddaughter on my mother's side, and she was receiving more attention. Gilian grew quickly; she was very talkative, and George did not like it at all, because Gilian was disturbing his peace.

At age sixteen, I left for the Netherlands to study. By this point, my parents had been divorced for three years—more about that coming up. During those turbulent years, I had understood I could choose to live with my father or my mother, and I chose my mother. The events that precipitated the divorce would impact my relationship with my father for many years.

While I lived in the Netherlands, my counsel to George focused on helping him be a good brother for his little sister—not to tease her and to take care of her.

"You are now the older brother in the house," I would say.

Once in a while, my mother would call me to ask me to talk to both of them, especially George. A peacemaker is someone who steps between two warring parties and initiates reconciliation after others have wronged them.

EMOTIONAL INTELLIGENCE

One book that had a great impact on me just before I left Curaçao for the Netherlands was *Emotional Intelligence: Why It Can Matter More Than IQ* by Daniel Goleman.

Goleman's EQ theory comprises five core components:

1. Empathy
2. Effective communication or social skills
3. Self-awareness
4. Self-regulation
5. Motivation

Shortly after reading *Emotional Intelligence*, I read *The Seven Habits of Highly Effective People* by Stephen Covey. The seven habits that he describes in the book are:

1. Be proactive, take responsibility for your life.
2. Begin with the end in mind.
3. Put first things first.
4. Think win-win.
5. Seek first to understand, then to be understood.

6. Synergize.
7. Sharpen the saw.

In chapters such as "Think Win-Win" and "Seek First to Understand, Then Be Understood," Covey describes the Indian talking stick, originally called a speaker's staff, a tool of indigenous democracy used by many tribes, especially those of the Northwest Coast in North America. The talking stick is passed around the group, allowing multiple people to speak in turn, and facilitates restorative conversations to ensure that participants are empowered and participating equally. Traditionally, talking sticks were used at major events, such as pow-wows, tribal council meetings and important ceremonies, but their use was also extended to storytelling circles, and teaching children. Talking sticks allow people to present and express their sacred point of view. Tribal leaders have also used it as a symbol of their authority and right to speak in public.

I was fascinated by this powerful metaphor of the talking stick, and I used it in my work as a team leader in 1998, whenever my team had a conflict. The first time I used this concept of the Indian talking stick was during a team meeting where I was the team leader of the interface and batch processes team. The team was responsible for information analysis, development, programming, and implementation of thirty-five interfaces to connect an old mainframe application of Delta Lloyd General Insurances with a new application. The project's implementation date was behind schedule, and the discussion was whether to reschedule; yes or no. It was an emotional meeting, and at one point, team members started yelling and insulting each other. It was a team of twenty FTE (full-time equivalents) from different disciplines: information analysts, programmers, and testers.

At a certain point, I felt the meeting getting out of control, and that was the first time I used the concept of the Indian talking stick. I stood up to get everyone's attention and asked everyone to be quiet. Then I showed them the pen I was holding in my hand and said, "This pen from now on is called the Indian talking stick."

I explained that the pen has "magical powers," because only the one who holds it is allowed to speak. Everyone else should remain silent and listen to the one speaking, not only with their ears but also with their hearts, trying to understand and feel the worries and pain of their teammates. Basically, this practice goes back to ancient times when villagers sat around the fire with the elder wisdom keepers. The one with more wisdom is the one who tells the stories to enrich and educate the younger ones. The word *shaman* derives from the word *samān* (from the Tungusic language), and it literally means, "The one who knows."

After I explained the talking stick's magical powers, the team fell silent. I asked who wanted to start, and we passed the stick around so everyone could speak up and express their concern. As the team leader, I summarized after every turn what the speaker had offered. Then I asked the other members if they understood what had been said. Turning to the member with the stick, I asked if we had understood him correctly. In the end, the worries, emotions, and risk of not reaching the deadline dissipated. The accusation that this had been a losing project because it had missed a deadline to go live was transformed into a creative and enthusiastic brainstorming session about what we could do to ensure the deadline was met. Everyone agreed that working Saturdays and Sundays for three to four weeks would definitely speed up the backlogs. So we began working on weekends. Ultimately the "go live" date was safeguarded.

This intervention with the talking stick truly enabled the skill of listening, which was being enhanced. Not having the stick means you have to listen; having to listen means seeking to understand first before being understood. To seek to understand before being understood, you need empathy, a healthy mind free of anger and jealousy.

Changing behavior and organizational culture takes time, but it starts with acknowledging the unacceptable behavior. If I look back through my childhood, youth, puberty, student years, and professional career, the common theme has always been a peacemaker. Sometimes I maintained harmony, and sometimes I took action whenever there was a fight or disturbance. Back then, the fights were with leaves, fists, and other relatively innocent weapons; now it is knives and other weapons.

PEACEMAKER IN MY OWN FAMILY

The year I was thirteen, my father returned from a business trip to St. Maarten, and I could sense that "his lamp was a bit loaded." That's an expression in our local language, Papiamentu, that means someone has been drinking.

On that Saturday night in May 1984, my brother, George, was nine and my sister, Gilian, four. My mother was dressed to go to a birthday party with two of her best friends, Atala and our Nanny Frida. My mother was waiting for my father to get home to take care of us so she could go to the party; it was around 7:30 p.m. I was in the kitchen—George and Gilian were in their bedrooms, asleep already.

From the kitchen where I was preparing toast for my evening meal, I heard my father arguing with my mother. They were standing in the living room. I could see and hear them clearly, because the only separation between the kitchen and the living room was the bar. I was not comfortable at all standing there in the kitchen, seeing and being part of their arguing. My peaceful environment was disrupted immediately. My father did not want my mother to go to the birthday party, and he became very aggressive. His tone was very hostile.

Knowing my mother's personality, this is the last tone you want to take with her because she will show no fear, no matter how great the threat. She will dig in her heels and do the opposite of what has been requested or dictated—in this specific case, my father telling her she couldn't go to the party.

"I just got home, and you cannot go to the party," my father said to my mother.

My mother said, *"Bou di ningun sirkuntansia mi no ta keda sin bai e fiesta,"* which meant that nothing was stopping her from going to that party. "I'm going to that party, Ibi—end of story."

My father grabbed my mother's hand and told her she was not

going. My mother made it clear again that she was going. Then, my father slapped my mother across her face.

I could not believe what I had just seen with my own eyes. How was it possible that my father had hit my mother? He was a calm and gentle man who had never shown signs of aggression. I was totally in shock. I started to cry slightly but suppressed most of the emotions going through my mind and body. My world had been turned upside down. I went straight to my room, where I then broke into tears. I cried heavily, and I cried for a couple of hours. My mother walked out the door without packing anything, heading straight to my grandmother's house.

Hearing my mother leave, I stayed in my room. I locked the door and cried for at least two hours. I could no longer look my father in the face. My father knocked on the door and asked me to open it. I told him to leave me alone. I did not want to talk to him. I was deeply hurt—I was broken into many pieces.

A few hours later, I heard my mother come home. I was still in a state of deep shock. I could not understand why my father behaved so strangely. My mother knocked on my door and asked me to open it. I opened the door for her, and she said, "Juny, Mommy is very sorry you had to see what happened between Mommy and Daddy, and that you saw how Daddy slapped Mommy in the face. Mommy went to Grandma's, and Mommy has decided that Mommy cannot live with Daddy anymore. Mommy is going to divorce Daddy."

I was speechless. I could understand her decision because both of them had educated us that aggression is never an alternative to solving any disagreement.

Just like that, my mother informed me she would divorce my father.

"You are thirteen years old, and you're allowed to choose where you want to live—with me or with your father."

She explained she would take care of George and Gilian because they were younger.

"I do not want to stay with my father," I said. "Where are we going to live?"

She told me we would temporarily live at my grandmother's house and that she would find a house to rent right away, so we could have our own house.

After that, she awakened George and Gilian to give them the news. George was quite happy—he asked my mother when he should start packing his things. Gilian was young and had no clue what was happening. There are two reasons George was happy. First of all, he and my dad always had a discussion about the kitchen, which was kind of my dad's favorite place in the house, but George loved to experiment in the kitchen too. Second, living at my grandmother's house would give him plenty of time to spend with my grandmother, and he was one of her favorite grandsons. My mother told us to start packing the next morning because we would be leaving soon.

I think we stayed for less than three days. The next day, one of my friends, who lived just two houses away, came to ask me what happened to me the night before because he could hear me crying from his room. I told him I was in great pain, but I did not tell him what had happened because I was ashamed.

The next day my father, who loves to cook, prepared a lunch of braised chicken and fried rice, setting the table with flowers for my mother. None of those actions could change the decision my mother had made the night before. My mother was a person of principle— once she made a decision, she would stick to it 1,000 percent. One of her favorite expressions to us was, *"Bo SI mester ta ta bo SI, bo NO mester ta bo NO,"* meaning that your yes should be a yes, your no should be a no, and once you say YES, stick to YES, and if you say NO, stick to NO. I could feel my father's embarrassment at the table during that lunch. My mother spoke not a word—she just sat at the table, taking bites of food. My father tried to convince her to stay by cooking a nice meal and buying flowers for her, but none of those gestures could change my mother's decision.

After we finished dinner, she told us to gather our things so we could go to my grandmother's house. One of my uncles, Anthony (Toontje) Juliana, drove up in his pickup. We took only our clothes, toys, and school materials, because my mother did not want to take anything else from the house.

"Leave everything else. I will buy everything we need for our new house," she said.

I said goodbye to my father, and we left for my grandmother's house, where she had prepared one of the larger rooms for us.

We did not stay for long. My mother, who knew many people through her employment as a nurse at the hospital, started to look for a home the day she told my father she was divorcing him. Within three to four weeks, she found a house for rent in the neighborhood of Montaña. During the summer of 1984, we moved from my grandmother's home in the neighborhood of Groot Kwartier to the neighborhood of Montaña, where we lived at Mehoranoweg #6. It was a nice house with spacious bedrooms, a kitchen, and a living room. We lived close to the Currie family, a popular family in the Montaña neighborhood, and we became very close friends.

After we moved out, contact with my father dwindled to almost zero. He visited us maybe once or twice at my grandmother's home and maybe four to five times at our house in Montaña. My mother felt protective of us as her children, and my father could not do anything to change her mind. I think she was so disappointed in my father, who was in her opinion the guilty one who ended their marriage, that she wanted to show him and the world she could raise us alone. That was a typical character trait of my mother—swimming against the current like salmon do. At that time, I just accepted my mother's belief that my father was the one responsible for the divorce, and she could raise us as a single parent.

For most of the rest of my childhood, I had virtually no contact with my father. When I embarked on my journey to the Netherlands to study chemical engineering and earn a bachelor's degree at the University of Amsterdam, I didn't have much of a relationship with him. From 1988 until 2003, when I returned to live on Curaçao, my contact with my father was almost zero. During summer vacations, when I came to Curaçao, I would visit him sometimes; but other times, I just ignored him. Divorce had severed the bond we had as father and son.

If there is one thing that I'm very glad I did before my father passed away in 2023, that one thing was to forgive him and ask him for forgiveness. Our lives are like a train—people get on the train, and people leave the train. The challenge is to make the train ride as pleasant as possible for all the passengers we have known in our lives. We do not know when we will reach our last stop and pass away, nor do we know when our fellow passengers will reach their last stop and pass away. It will be painful if someone in our life passes away, and we still have so many questions to ask or unfinished topics to discuss.

We are not human beings in search of a spiritual experience—we are spiritual beings immersed in a human life. That means we are all connected to each other and should love each other. My life train and that of my father had derailed for almost thirty-four years. Now I'm happy and at peace that our train got back on track in 2017/2018 and that we could spend his last five years as close friends, learning everything that he still wanted us to learn. I was also able to be with him during his last breath and helped him with his transition from this physical world to the spirit realm. The circle of life was closed; he was at peace, and I was at peace.

Part II

How Unhealthy Minds Create Unhealthy Nations

CHAPTER 7

First Trauma

Unhealthy minds definitely will result in an unhealthy nation. It doesn't matter what the origin or cause of the unhealthy mind is. A personal experience or an intergenerational experience, it defines how we think, how we speak, how we act, and it will define our characters, and our future. In my personal case, it was physical abuse of my mother (a slap on her face) that had a long-lasting consequence on my thoughts and feelings toward my father, for decades—without knowing it could have had a long-lasting effect on my heart condition, which was cleared during my first retreat in Los Lobos Sanctuary in Chile.

Now imagine the brutal effect of transatlantic slavery, where children, men, and women were ripped apart from their families, forced onto a boat, and shipped like cattle to a new location where they had never been before; more or less the same weather conditions, but far away from their home. In their new home, somewhere in the Americas or the Caribbean, the slaves were forced to work under labor conditions that Human Rights organizations nowadays would definitely shut down each and every operation or company that did exploit humans in such a barbaric way.

Consider the huge impact it had on me watching my mother get slapped in the face compared to the brutal conditions of transatlantic slavery. Witnessing my mother's slap in the face and transatlantic slavery can be categorized as Adverse Childhood Experiences (often called ACEs). ACEs are potentially traumatic events that happen before the age of eighteen, in my case, at the age of thirteen. They can have a lasting impact on a person's health, development, and overall well-being. The concept stems from the CDC–Kaiser Permanente ACE Study (1995–1997), which demonstrated a strong association between childhood adversity and later-life health outcomes. There are three categories of ACEs: 1. Abuse, 2. Neglect, 3. Household dysfunction.

1. Abuse
   A. Physical abuse
   B. Emotional abuse
   C. Sexual abuse
2. Neglect
   A. Physical neglect (not having enough food, clean clothes, shelter, etc.)
   B. Emotional neglect (not feeling loved, supported, or cared for)
3. Household Dysfunction
   A. Substance abuse in the household
   B. Mental illness in the household
   C. Domestic violence
   D. Parental separation or divorce
   E. Incarcerated household member

WHY DOES ACES MATTER?

Higher ACE scores (the number of different ACEs a child experiences) are linked to greater risks of:

- Chronic health problems (heart disease, diabetes, cancer)
- Mental health issues (depression, anxiety, PTSD)
- Risky behaviors (substance misuse, unsafe sex)
- Lower educational and occupational achievement

ACEs can affect brain development, stress-response systems, and even gene expression through toxic stress. Not everyone with ACEs develops negative outcomes. Having supportive relationships, community resources, healthy coping skills, trauma-informed care, and healing can buffer the effects and promote resilience.

UNHEALTHY NATIONS

To uncover the seeds of an unhealthy nation, we need to go deeper into the layers of wounds that created the nation's mindset. This history has had a human cost, with an impact felt in the individual mind and the collective mind. In this chapter, I will talk specifically about the lessons I learned on my native island of Curaçao: ENNIA, Refinery and Hospital. It is my hope that these powerful lessons will inspire you to become a more active citizen of your own country, a citizen with a calm mind, a citizen with a healthy mind, and a citizen who has tapped into their own inner light!

My home country, Curaçao, like many nations in the Caribbean and the Americas, has been shaped by slavery, colonialism, and the culture of its indigenous inhabitants. In her book *Post Traumatic Slave Syndrome: America's Legacy of Enduring Injury and Healing*, Dr. Joy DeGruy describes the effect of chattel slavery and the traumas affecting contemporary life in the Caribbean and the Americas. Many behaviors of Afro-Americans are being examined through the lens of the legacy of slavery. Post-traumatic slave syndrome—let's just consider this term for a minute. DeGruy defines it as "a condition that exists when a population has experienced multigenerational trauma resulting from centuries of slavery and continues to experience oppression and institutionalized racism today."

Trauma is when we experience stressful, frightening, or distressing events that are difficult to cope with or are out of our control. It could be a single incident or an ongoing event that lasts over a long period of time. Most of us will experience an event in our lives that could be considered traumatic.

One particular example of a traumatic experience that shapes the behavior of our thoughts, habits, character, and destiny, which is not only applicable in America, but also in Curaçao, is the following example from her book:

> It is equally understandable why an African American might feel threatened by the accomplishments of a peer when viewed in the light of slavery. Slaves were divided in many different respects; masters distinguished the house slave from the field slave, the mulatto from the black slave, etc. Often these different designations meant access to, or denial of, privileges and sometimes freedom itself. It was common practice for slave owners to set one class of slave against another. Slave owners perpetuated feelings of separateness and distrust by sometimes ordering black overseers to beat or punish their friends, peers and relatives. When the master "promoted" a slave, that slave often joined the master in the rank of oppressor.

The behavior of feeling threatened and the lack of collaboration are still prevalent in Curaçaoan society and can be labeled as "Crab in a barrel syndrome." Crab in a barrel syndrome (also called crab mentality) is a metaphor for a self-defeating behavior found in groups, in which individuals try to pull down or obstruct the progress of others who are succeeding, rather than supporting them. The term comes from the way crabs behave in a bucket; when one crab tries to climb out, the others pull it back down, ensuring that none escape. In human behavior, this syndrome describes situations, such as:

- People discouraging or criticizing others for achieving success
- Jealousy or resentment toward someone who stands out or improves their circumstances
- A collective mindset that says, "if I can't have it, neither should you," an unhealthy mindset

Together, these three factors—slavery, colonialism, and the marginalization of indigenous culture—have shaped the collective unconscious of Curaçao. These unhealthy mind habits have affected the national mindset, and the effects are present to this day, both in shared public life, and the culture, as well as at the family and individual level.

THE ORIGIN OF TRANSATLANTIC SLAVERY

How did it all start? What was the origin of transatlantic slavery? First, you divide the world in half. In the fifteenth century, the Roman Catholic Church divided the world in half, granting Portugal a monopoly on trade in West Africa, and in Spain, the right to colonize the New World in its quest for land and gold. Pope Nicholas V buoyed Portuguese efforts and issued the Romanus Pontifex of 1455, which affirmed Portugal's exclusive rights to territories it claimed along the West African coast and the trade from those areas. It granted the right to invade, plunder, and "reduce their persons to perpetual slavery."

Queen Isabella of Spain invested in Christopher Columbus's exploration to increase her wealth and ultimately rejected the enslavement of Native Americans, claiming they were Spanish subjects. Spain established an *asiento*, or contract, that authorized the direct shipment of captive Africans for trade as human commodities in the Spanish colonies in the Americas. Eventually other European nation-states—the Netherlands, France, Denmark, and England—seeking similar economic and geopolitical power, joined in the trade. They exchanged goods and people with leaders along the West African coast, who ran self-sustaining societies known for their mineral-rich land and wealth in gold and other trade goods. They competed to secure the *asiento* and colonize the New World. With these efforts, a new form of slavery came into being.

It was endorsed by the European nation-states and based on race, and it resulted in the largest forced migration in the world. Some 12.5 million men, women, and children of African descent were forced into the trans-Atlantic slave trade. The sale of their bodies and the product of their labor brought the Atlantic world into being, including colonial North America, the Caribbean, and South America. In the colonies, status was defined by race and class, and whether by custom, case law, or statute, freedom was limited to maintain the enterprise of slavery and ensure power. The key here is that leaders along the West African coast who ran self-sustaining societies due to their mineral-rich land and wealth in gold and other trade goods exchanged goods and people with European nations, and in some cases, their own people

Exchanging goods and people. As long as the human race has existed, there have been unhealthy minds; unhealthy minds that die to power and later on, money, not taking into account the general interest but only their self-interest. Abraham Lincoln said, "Nearly all men can stand adversity, but if you want to test a man's character, give him power."

The cumulative effect of all these unhealthy minds is that our world is suffering. At the same time, it presents an opportunity. Whenever there is collective pain or suffering, we have a chance to grow and search for the light within.

Plato once said, "Only those who do not seek power are qualified to hold it." In basic terms, Plato's Theory of Forms holds that the physical world is not the "real" world—instead, ultimate reality exists beyond our physical world. What is blocking our minds so we cannot experience oneness? How do we not see that all human beings are equal, independently of race, religion, and social status? What is forming our thoughts, emotions, and actions to have the need for "power" at the cost of others? I would say it's a drama of archetypes—the triangle of victim, rescuer, and persecutor.

THE TRIANGLE OF VICTIM, RESCUER, AND PERSECUTOR

Granting Portugal a monopoly on trade in West Africa and in Spain, the right to colonize the New World in its quest for land and gold is a political machination. Granting a monopoly, granting the right to invade, plunder, and reduce persons to perpetual slavery creates a triangle—victim (the slave), rescuer (the priest/religion), and persecutor (the colonialist). This is an archetypal dynamic in which the fundamental aspects of human spirituality are violated—relationship, values, and life purpose. The shamans, healers, sages, and wisdom keepers of all times, all continents, and all peoples in their ageless wisdom firmly believed that these three fundamental aspects were necessary for human spiritual evolution.

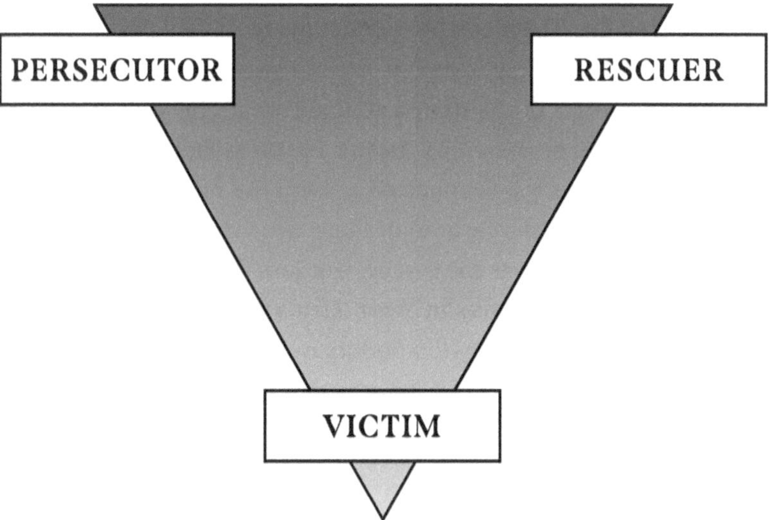

Figure 3: The triangle of victim, rescuer, and persecutor

About forty years ago, Stephen Karpman, MD, developed the drama triangle—victim, rescuer, persecutor. I find it's just as relevant—and just as new to many people—as it was then. This triangle can also be applied to slavery four hundred years ago.

Even if you don't spend much time yourself playing any of these three roles, you probably deal daily with people who do. Knowing how to put our "big girl" or "big boy" pants on and get out of the triangle is essential when dealing with people who want to pull us in. Using our wise mind to recognize when we've regressed into one of these roles ourselves (usually because of the usual culprit, needing to play those roles early in our family-of-origin conditioning) is also essential to make wise conscious choices in our intimate and social interactions with others.

The drama triangle is a dynamic model of social interaction and conflict developed by Karpman, a student of Eric Berne, MD, the father of transactional analysis. Karpman and other clinicians point out that "victim, rescuer, and persecutor" refer to roles people unconsciously play, or try to manipulate others into playing, not to the actual circumstances in someone's life. There can be real victims of slavery, crime, racism, or abuse, and these victims can go on from generation to generation.

The three roles of the drama triangle are archetypal and easily recognizable in their extreme versions. For the island of Curaçao, the three roles can easily be connected to both the natives of the island of Curaçao and the slaves; both of them were **victims**. The priest or the Catholic Church was **the rescuer** because the beliefs/ceremonies of the natives or the slaves in West Africa and the Americas were characterized as black magic/voodoo, or witchery. The colonizers are **the persecutors**.

Victims

The victim's stance is "poor me!" Victims see themselves as victimized, oppressed, powerless, helpless, hopeless, dejected, and ashamed, and come across as "super-sensitive," wanting kid-glove treatment from others. They can deny any responsibility for their negative circumstances and claim they lack the power to change those circumstances. A person in the victim role will look for a rescuer, a savior, to save them (and if someone refuses or fails to do so, they can quickly perceive that person as a persecutor). In terms of derailing resilience, victims have real difficulties making decisions, solving problems, finding much pleasure in life, or understanding their self-perpetuating behaviors.

Both the native inhabitants and the slave population of Curaçao have been victims for many centuries.

Rescuers

The stance of the rescuer is "Let me help you!" Rescuers work hard to help and caretake other people, even going so far as to help them feel good about themselves, while neglecting their own needs or failing to take responsibility for meeting them. Rescuers are classically codependent and enablers. They need victims to help and often can't allow the victim to succeed or get better. They can use guilt to keep their victims dependent and feel guilty themselves if they are not rescuing somebody. In terms of derailing resilience, rescuers are frequently harried, overworked, and tired, caught in a martyrdom style, while resentment festers beneath the surface. The basic beliefs, practices, and ceremonies of both the slaves and the natives were characterized as black magic, voodoo, or witchery. For the South American native inhabitants, it was mandatory to convert to Christianity by the Spanish, and the Spanish conquerors and the slaves from Africa converted to Christianity by the European conquerors.

Persecutors

The stance of the persecutor is "It's all your fault!" Persecutors criticize and blame the victim, set strict limits, can be controlling, rigid, authoritative, angry, and unpleasant. They keep the victim feeling oppressed through threats and bullying. In terms of resilience, persecutors can't bend, can't be flexible, can't be vulnerable, and can't be human; they fear becoming victims themselves. Persecutors yell and criticize, but they don't actually solve any problems or help anyone else solve the problem. These are the extreme versions of these three roles, but we encounter people playing milder versions of them regularly. The Spanish, Portuguese, Dutch, French, and British have been persecutors during the transatlantic slave period.

What gives the drama triangle much of its power and significance is the recognition that people will switch roles and cycle through all three roles without ever getting out of the triangle. Victims depend on a savior; rescuers yearn for a basket case; persecutors need a scapegoat. The trap is that people are acting out these roles to meet personal (often unconscious) needs rather than seeing the picture as a whole and taking responsibility for their part in keeping the triangle going. Curaçao, for example, is still feeling the effects.

EFFECTS ON CURAÇAO

Curaçao as a nation has many collective healthy and unhealthy national mindsets. We are creative, pragmatic, resourceful, and talented in sports and music. These are healthy national mindsets. But Curaçao also has other unconscious national behaviors like envy, jealousy, and lack of togetherness (unhealthy national mindset). Our community pride is deeply rooted in our history—and our roles as victims, rescuers, and persecutors. For instance, the lack of collaboration still plays an important role in the Curaçaon society. For an island of approximately 155,823, according to the 2023 census, with a Parliamentary democracy, Curaçao has eight political parties that participated in the last election in March 2025, compared to fifteen (as of the latest election in March 2021). The Parliament, which consists of twenty-one members and was formed after the elections of March 2025, is represented by eight parties, and a minimum of eleven members is required to form the government. This structure was introduced four hundred years ago by the colonizers to divide and conquer. The divisive effect is still present in our society today, and it disrupts the real progress of Curaçao. In the next section, I will share a few examples of the effects of historically unhealthy mindsets on Curacao, as well as ways that unhealthy nations like my own can change their trajectory and start healing.

On May 13, 1990, Pope John Paul II arrived in Curaçao for a one-day visit. A large crowd assembled at Hato, the international airport, to greet him. During his public address, he blessed the people of Curaçao from the balcony at the governor's palace in Willemstad. The highlight of the visit was the celebration of a Mass at the sports stadium in Brievengat, attended by almost 16,000 people.

Catholicism was and remains the main religion of Curaçao, introduced by Spanish conquistadors. Every indigenous inhabitant of the Curaçao island had to convert to Catholicism. The same goes for every slave who was transferred to Curaçao. Catholicism is deeply rooted in Curaçao.

But what was wrong with the beliefs and the practice of spirituality of the Arawak people? What was wrong with the beliefs and the practice of spirituality of the transatlantic slaves who brought their traditions from West Africa? What was wrong with these beliefs and traditions, and why was Catholicism not wrong?

In his book *The Arawak: The History and Legacy of the Indigenous Natives in South America and the Caribbean*, Charles River Editors offers a concise exploration of the Arawak people, focusing on their culture, history, and interactions with European colonizers. The Arawak people had a rich spiritual and religious tradition deeply rooted in shamanism. Their belief system was animistic, meaning they viewed the world as inhabited by benevolent and malevolent spirits. Shamans, or spiritual leaders, played a crucial role in mediating between the physical and spiritual realms through rituals, ceremonies, and healing practices.

On one hand, Catholicism gives faith and hope, but on the other hand, religion has wiped out the indigenous wisdom, such as shamanism, that was already present on the island and practiced by both the Arawak and the descendants of slavery from West Africa. What kind of mind wipes out a complete spiritual and religious tradition, imposing its own religion?

CURAÇAO'S NATIONAL FLAG

The design of the flag of a nation reveals how healthy or unhealthy its mindset is. Does it reveal pain and suffering, or does it reveal hope, faith, love, and healing? The flag of Curaçao depicts the sea, the sun, the sky, and the land, powerful symbols of Mother Earth. That's the strength and energy level of the island, which will be explained later in Chapter 8; it has a unique history and great healing energies.

The national flag was designed by Martin den Dulk in 1984. The government of Curaçao organized a competition to select a national flag that would represent the island. Martin den Dulk was one of many participants, but his interpretation of the flag won over judges. He won the competition, and his flag became the national flag of Curaçao. The blue background of the flag symbolizes the sea and the sky. The yellow band represents the bright sun, which bathes the islands. The two stars in the left-hand corner represent Curaçao and Klein Curaçao, the much smaller uninhabited island southeast of Curaçao that is part of the country of Curaçao.

Figure 4: National flag of Curaçao

In 1983, a new office called Sede di Papiamentu (SdP) was founded in Curaçao. It provided retraining for primary school teachers, and was tasked with developing a provisional language-teaching method called *"Papiamentu nos Idioma"* (Papiamentu Our Language). As a result, Papiamentu was introduced as a compulsory subject, to be taught for thirty minutes a day across all primary classes in the educational school system, starting in 1986. Recognizing and introducing Papiamentu as a compulsory subject was an important and historic moment. Unhealthy minds/unhealthy nations wipe out indigenous languages. When nations are on their way to regain their health, it's because of healthy minds. Teaching children in their native language has several benefits, including:

1. **Stronger Cognitive Development.** Learning in a language they understand helps children develop critical thinking and problem-solving skills more effectively.

2. **Better Academic Performance.** Students grasp concepts more easily, leading to higher achievement in subjects like math, science, and reading.

3. **Increased Confidence and Participation.** Children are more likely to engage in class discussions and express their ideas when learning in a familiar language.

4. **Stronger Cultural Identity.** Using their native language helps children stay connected to their culture, traditions, and family heritage.

5. **Easier Transition to Additional Languages.** A strong foundation in the native language makes it easier to learn a second or third language later.

6. **Improved Literacy Skills.** Children who first develop literacy in their native language tend to become better readers and writers in other languages.

7. **Better Communication with Family and Community.** Maintaining their native language allows children to interact meaningfully with parents, grandparents, and others in their community.

According to the 2023 census conducted by the Central Bureau of Statistics Curaçao, there are 60,125 private households on the island. While census data indicates that 78 percent of the population primarily speaks Papiamentu at home, it does not specify the exact number of households where Papiamentu is the primary language. Therefore, based on the available information, we can estimate that approximately 78 percent of the 60,125 households, which is about 46,898 households, primarily use Papiamentu at home. This estimation aligns with the data presented in the 2023 census results.

Several scientific studies support the benefits of teaching children in their native language. In an article commemorating UNESCO's annual celebration of International Mother Language Day, it is noted that mother-language-based education is essential, according to www.unesco.org.

One notable activist in this regard is poet, novelist, and language advocate Frank Martinus Arion, who moved to the Netherlands in 1955 and returned to Curaçao in 1981, where he became the director of the Curaçao Language Institute that promoted the use of the native language, Papiamentu. His works include *De laatste vrijheid (The Last Freedom)* and *Dubbelspel (Double Play)*. The latter novel is considered his magnum opus and was published in 1973. It was also turned into a movie in 2017. He wrote both in Papiamentu and in Dutch.

THE INFLUENCE OF SPORTS

Sports play a crucial role in the development of a nation by influencing various aspects of society, including health, economy, social cohesion, and international reputation. Here are some key impacts.

Health and Well-Being

- Encourages physical activity, reducing lifestyle diseases like obesity, diabetes, and heart disease.
- Promotes mental health by reducing stress, anxiety, and depression.

- Enhances discipline, teamwork, and resilience, fostering a healthier and more productive population.

Economic Growth

- Sports generate jobs in areas such as coaching, event management, sports medicine, and media.
- Increases tourism through international sporting events like the Olympics or the World Cup.
- Encourages investment in infrastructure, such as stadiums and fitness centers, boosting local economies.

Social Cohesion and National Unity

- Brings people together across different social, ethnic, and economic backgrounds.
- Promotes national pride and identity, especially during international competitions.
- Provides an avenue for youth engagement, reducing crime, and social unrest.

Education and Youth Development

- Encourages discipline, teamwork, and leadership skills among young people.
- Helps students perform better academically by improving focus and discipline.
- Offers scholarships and career opportunities in professional sports.

International Recognition and Diplomacy

- Enhances a country's image on the global stage through successful athletes and teams.

- Strengthens diplomatic relations through sports exchange programs and international competitions.
- Acts as a platform for cultural exchange and soft-power diplomacy.

Sports are an area where Curaçao always excels, thanks to the many talents on the island. Even in soccer, many local players or players with local roots like Patrick Kluivert (Ajax and FC Barcelona) and Leroy Fer (Feyenoord and Norwich City) have played in the World Cup for the Netherlands rather than for Curaçao. I strongly believe Curaçao can qualify for the World Cup, which will have an enormous impact on the island from a nation-building perspective. The 2026 World Cup edition in Mexico, the USA, and Canada brings such a unique opportunity for the Concacaf region, of which Curaçao is part. This is because instead of three national teams, a total of eight national teams could qualify for the World Cup 2026 for the Concacaf region, consisting of these three hosting countries: Mexico, USA, and Canada—three national teams from the qualifying round and two national teams from the knockout round, which will take place in March 2026. Given the significant potential spin-off, it is imperative that as a nation we do everything we can to qualify for the World Cup 2026, and I'm supporting the efforts to make this happen. As of April 10, 2025, I have been elected as the President of Curaçao Football Federation, where I can be of service in the development of the local soccer competition and create the framework conditions for the national team to perform optimally with one common goal: to qualify the Curaçao men's national soccer team for the first time to a World Cup edition.

CURAÇAO NOWADAYS

Curaçao is one of the three autonomous countries of the Kingdom of the Netherlands (with Aruba and Saint-Martin). It has a constitution (Dutch: *staatsregelingen*) that governs its constitutional organization and has been approved by law (Dutch: *landverordening*) adopted by a two-thirds' majority of the local parliament, in application of Chapter IV of the Charter for the Kingdom of the Netherlands (Dutch: Statuut voor het Koninkrijk der Nederlanden), dating from 1954 and reformed in 2010. The Constitution of Curaçao (Dutch: *Staatsregeling* van Curaçao; *Papiamento: Konstitushon di Kòrsou*) was adopted by a fifteen-to-six majority vote in the island council of Curaçao on September 5, 2010. In the initial vote on the constitution in July, the two-thirds majority required was not reached, after which new elections were held on August 27, 2010. The newly elected island council could then adopt the constitution with an ordinary majority. The constitution entered into force on October 10, 2010, on the date of the dissolution of the Netherlands Antilles.

As indicated in the introduction of this chapter, Curaçao has national characteristics that can be described as healthy individual and collective mindsets like creativeness, pragmatism, and resourcefulness. Curaçao is talented in sports and music, and as of February 2024, Curaçao has seventeen players who have played in Major League Baseball, of which are four active players: Ozzie Albies and Jurickson Profar from the Atlanta Braves, Kenley Jansen from the Detroit Tigers, and Ceddanne Rafaela from the Boston Red Sox. With a total population of 155,823, 0.155 million and two starters on opening day 2023 in the MLB (data from Bat Digest), this is approximately 0.013 per 1,000 (2/156 = 0.0128). A comparison with other Caribbean islands for the starters on opening day 2023 shows the following data:

- Puerto Rico; population of 3.2 million; eight starters on opening day 2023; 0.0025 per 1,000,
- Dominican Republic; population of 11.5 million, twenty-seven starters on opening day 2023, 0.0023 per 1,000.
- Cuba; population of 11.34 million; fourteen starters on opening day 2023; 0.0012 per 1,000.

Starters means those in the starting batting lineup on opening day in that analysis; actual total MLB players ever from every country will be higher. Curaçao shows a much higher ratio (0.013 per 1,000) compared to the larger Caribbean countries. This reflects how a very small population but a few very high-profile MLB players lifts the per-capita figure.

There are collective unhealthy national mindsets that are unconscious, but the results of these behaviors have been noticed in the last decades. For example, the murder of politician, Helmin Wiels, on May 5, 2013, the first prime minister of the country Curaçao, Gerrit Schotte, was sentenced to three years in prison in March 2016 for bribery and money laundering, committed when he was in office as Prime Minister from October 2010 to September 2012. Envy and jealousy deprives us of working together as a country. It's amazing how character assassination is being designed and executed against any individuals who excel in general interest, sincerity, openness, and honesty. There are behaviors and forces of our collective unconscious that are not yet open to purity, abundance, and love; they're based instead on scarcity and envy. This collective unconsciousness goes all the way back to the origins of slavery in West Africa, and it disrupts the progress of Curaçao.

Not only that, but also the drama triangle affects Curaçao to this day: the slaves/natives (the victims), the rescuers (the priests), and the colonizers (Spain, England, and the Netherlands). Even the slaves switched from their victim role of the rescuer of colonizers when the master "promoted" a slave, and that slave often joined the master in the rank of oppressor/persecutor.

We have been victims, rescuers, and persecutors for centuries. I admit, I have been in the victim part of the triangle for more than thirty years. A victim of observing my father giving my mother a slap in her face, which was a traumatic experience for a child of my age. A victim of the divorce of my parents, a victim of an adolescent growing up without a father. A victim of emotions that made it difficult to forgive my father for what he had done to my mother and to his children. A victim who is unconsciously jealous of other children who have grown up in a good relationship with both parents.

CHAPTER 8

Why Does National History Matter

Childhood trauma can have lasting impacts, affecting our decisions even as adults. So, to develop a healthy mindset, you must gain awareness of how your history and your nation's history influence your beliefs.

In 1988, I was about to leave Curaçao for the Netherlands to attend university. I would learn more about how my personal traumatic experience at age twelve had harmed my behaviors and thoughts, as well as my feelings toward my father. I was also about to find out how the trauma of one nation, particularly a colonizer, can impact the mind of another. I had grown up in a Dutch colony—now I was going to the source.

Before I left the island of Curaçao, I made three promises to myself:

- I will be successful in the Netherlands so my mother, father, brother, and sister will be proud of me. I will be an example for my brother and sister.
- I will be a good husband when the time comes for marriage.

- I will be a good father to my children, even in case of a possible divorce, which I did not hope for, of course. I will make sure my children have a strong relationship with their mother, because I did not want them to experience what I did.

To be all of that, to comply with all those promises I made to myself, I had to be flexible and adapt to setbacks in life, which I could not have foreseen before starting this journey but which I have learned to deal with and mastered along the way. I couldn't have foreseen that I would have my first spiritual experience in Amsterdam. What was at stake for me from the transition of living on the small island of Curaçao to the Netherlands? What would I be exposed to that I should overcome? What would be the mundane temptations? What would be the spiritual lesson?

My journey started on August 8, 1988. I can remember that day as if it were today. Many friends and relatives of my mother asked her if it was a wise decision to let me leave for the Netherlands at age sixteen. I had finished high school in Curaçao early. I was a young man seeking opportunities, and the Netherlands was a country of many opportunities—you can become a known professor, but you can also become a known criminal.

LAND OF OPPORTUNITY

What do I mean by "you can become a known professor, but you can also become a known criminal?" I have seen a young high school student from Curaçao drive a brand-new Porsche in Amsterdam; shortly after, he was arrested. The Netherlands provides both opportunities, so it's up to you which road you choose. The Netherlands has a notorious history in terms of drugs. In the nineteenth century, it was a leading producer of cocaine. Today, it is plagued by synthetic drugs. But the Netherlands is also a leader in education and many other positive conditions from a social point of view.

My biggest dream as a child was to study medicine to become a doctor. I wanted to be a pathologist-anatomist. My second choice was to be a gynecologist. Since I finished Higher General Education at Peter Stuyvesant College, I could not be admitted directly to the universities in the Netherlands to study medicine, which left me with two options. I could finish an advanced science education in Curaçao, or I could obtain a first-year certification of bachelor studies in the Netherlands, which gives me the right to be admitted for a master study.

A third challenge presented itself: In the Netherlands, the master program of study in medicine was a *"numerus fixus programme."* For some study programs, the educational institution has set a certain capacity. This means that a limited number of places are available. This is called *"numerus fixus."* If the number of students who apply exceeds the number of available places, a selection procedure will take place. To be admitted to a master's program to study medicine if you are from the island of Curaçao, you would have to petition the government of Curaçao for a so-called "minister place." A minister's place gains you the right to enter the program to study medicine at any university in the Netherlands if you have an advanced science education diploma.

It takes five years to earn a Higher General Education diploma and six years to earn an Advanced Science Education diploma. Due to my excellent grades, I had the option to go directly to the sixth level of Advanced Science Education, take the exam, petition for a minister place, and then depart the next year (1989) to the Netherlands to study medicine. But I decided to go to the Netherlands to study after finishing Higher General Education, obtain in one year the certification of a bachelor study, then apply to enter the study of medicine. This choice was mainly driven because our mother always told us to be independent and surely independent of politics. For me, it was a no-go to ask for anything. I would do it on my own force.

So I applied for the study of Higher Laboratory Education, a bachelor study at the University of Amsterdam, at that time Hogeschool van Amsterdam, to obtain my first-year certification, which would allow me to start with the master program of medicine the next year. I was excellent in chemistry, mathematics, biology, and physics. Almost all high school students who finish high school in the Netherlands receive a scholarship.

Upon my arrival in Amsterdam in 1998, my uncle Raymond helped me unpack my luggage and showed me around the building, the neighborhood, and the shopping area of Buikslotermeerplein, which was within a five-minute walk: a shopping area in Amsterdam North. There was a huge supermarket, C-1000, where I could buy groceries. My uncle showed me everything I needed to start my life as a student in Amsterdam. A week later, he asked another friend to show me how to navigate public transportation to get to my classes, which would start in September. So, I still had a couple of weeks to get used to my new life in Amsterdam.

MY FIRST SPIRITUAL EXPERIENCE

The first night in my room was when I had my initial spiritual experience. It shocked me for weeks. I was sleeping, and it was past midnight. Suddenly I began to sweat. I got goose bumps, and my body froze. My bed sat in the middle of the room. I was positioned on the bed with my head toward the window of the room. I struggled to turn my head. I was paralyzed. After a couple of minutes, I could clearly sense footsteps on my bed. I could feel the mattress pressing in next to my legs. I was terrified. It was the first time in my life that I sensed the presence of a spiritual being. I kept looking toward the window and observed the shadow of a human being, but without legs, floating toward the window. The place close to my legs where the mattress was pressed down released, but still I could not move. This shadow stayed at the window for a couple of minutes, then turned around and looked at me with deep penetrating eyes. It floated over my bed toward the entrance and left. After a couple of minutes, I could start moving again. I stopped sweating and the goose bumps disappeared.

After that, I could not sleep anymore, so I called my mother. She called my grandmother, who was clairvoyant, and she told me that it was the soul of someone who had lived in that room before but died in an accident in that area and did not have a proper funeral. The entity was still wandering around. She advised me to pray for a proper transition to the spiritual world for that specific soul. And I should clean the room with incense and garlic.

I did exactly what I had been told, and I never saw that shadow again. However, it took me weeks before I could sleep normally again in my own room. That was my first spiritual experience with a spiritual being ever, and it almost became a traumatic experience. Thanks to my mother and grandmother, I understood what had happened and what should have been done to help this soul cross over to the spiritual world.

My spiritual lesson in the first year of living in the Netherlands empowered my moral compass. Being exposed to all those mundane temptations that Amsterdam and the Netherlands have to offer—drugs, women, sex/prostitution, a view of the spiritual realm, and the suffering of a soul that has left this world tragically and is still dwarfing around trying to find someone who could help with the transition to the spirit realm. This definitely strengthened my moral compass, distinguishing between right and wrong, and doing the right things regardless of the consequences.

A SURPRISING OFFER

After the first year, still with the ambition of getting admitted to the University of Amsterdam to study medicine, I did not qualify for all my required credits to obtain the bachelor certification of the first year, which would grant entrance to the master program of medicine. I decided to do the first year all over again to improve my grades with a minimum average of eight, which was a requirement to be admitted for the master program of medicine, that's a *numerus fixus* program. After the second year, my grades improved, and I applied for the master program of medicine, but I was not admitted. I then decided to continue and finish the study of Higher Laboratory Education, which I finished in June 1993.

By this time, I was twenty-one and thought I was too young to start working, so I continued with the master program of chemistry at the University of Amsterdam. Then I chose the graduate program in chemical engineering. My dream of becoming a doctor was not coming together, so I switched to study what I also loved, which was chemistry, with the ambition to one day return to Curaçao and work at the refinery, at that time operated by PDVSA, the Venezuelan oil company.

The faculty of chemistry and economics of the University of Amsterdam was at Roeter Island, a small area close to Roeterstreet, which they call Roeter Island in Amsterdam. The history of the Roeter Island campus goes back further than the twentieth century. Roeterseiland has been busy for centuries. In the seventeenth century, the city began a major urban expansion that would become world famous: the ring of canals. That ring of canals had to accommodate the large influx of immigrants who wanted to live in the capital. After several decades, however, Amsterdam's appeal proved not to be as great as was anticipated, leaving some parts empty. "Roeterseiland was the center of brandy distilleries in the seventeenth century." On those undeveloped sections of the canal belt, space was made for trade, warehouses, and small factories. The Roeterseiland became the center of brandy distilleries. Ideally, the residual products of the wine distilleries could directly serve the animals on Pig Island, located a little further west (between the Amstel and the present-day Wibautstraat). In addition to alcohol producers, the Roeterseiland also housed a glassworks and an iron foundry.

On one of those canals, *"Nieuwe achtergacht,"* meaning the "New back canal," there are a couple of billiard pubs. Students from the faculty of economics and chemistry would visit the pubs after college for social gatherings. I remember clearly in the spring of 1994, I went to one of those billiard pubs with a couple of other students, something I never did because I do not like the environment of bars and pubs. We would stay for a maximum of one hour, just to discuss one of the projects of chemical reactor engineering. I was the only dark-colored student—all the other students were from the Netherlands. Just in front of us was another table, and I could hear three men speaking in Spanish. I was the only one in my group who could understand.

To go to the toilet, you had to pass close to their table, and as I did, one of them approached me, saying, "Good afternoon," which I took to mean, where are you from?

"I'm from Curaçao," I responded.

"Then you can speak and understand Spanish," he said.

"Yes, I can," I said.

He switched to Spanish. "*Ustedes son estudiantes?*" he asked, which means, "Are you students?"

"*Si, somos estudiantes*," I replied, which means, "Yes, we are students."

"*Que estan estudiando?*" he said, which means, "What are you studying?"

Without knowing their intention, I said, "*Estamos estudiando ingeniería química*," or "We are studying chemistry engineering."

"*Muy interesante, nosotros somos de Colombia, sabes cuanto le pagan a un químico que trabaja para los carteles mensualmente*," he said, which translates as, "Very interesting, do you know how much they pay a chemist working for drug cartels in Colombia on a monthly basis." He added before I could answer. "*El pago mensual es de US$60.000*," which means, "The monthly payment is $60.000." "*Tienes interes*," he said, or "Are you interested?"

I was shocked and responded immediately with "*No muchas gracias*," or no. I kept walking.

When I returned to the table with my friends, I informed the other students that we should leave and choose another place to meet. That is when it became obvious to me that drug cartels were recruiting chemistry students to work for them in Colombia. It had not even crossed my mind that this was possible—the values from my upbringing had spared me from much misery. Amsterdam is a city with both good and bad sides. It's up to you which one you will choose. My upbringing and the teachings of both my mother and father were immediately activated when I received that "surprising offer." I was taught there are no shortcuts for becoming financially independent. You have to study, and you have to work hard. So everything in my body said no to this surprising offer.

CHAPTER 9

The Impact of Traumatic Events on the Mind, Brain, and Body

Throughout the history of humanity, we have had to deal with both unforeseen events and events we have created ourselves, with devastating results. In our history, we carry a slate of traumatic events.[1]

The worldwide influenza pandemic in 1918 killed approximately fifty million people. By comparison, the COVID-19 pandemic from 2020 to 2023 killed approximately seven million people. Both can be denominated as unforeseen events, although there have been plenty of theories that we created the coronavirus. The Black Death pandemic between 1347 and 1351 killed an estimated seventy-five to 200 million people in Eurasia.

The transatlantic slave trade, however, was not an unforeseen event—it was created by humankind. It was legally sanctioned, allowing imperialist nations to conquer and enslave Africans and transport

---

1   Elkhonon Goldberg, *The Executive Brain: Frontal Lobes and the Civilized Mind* (Oxford University Press, 2001).

them in horrible conditions to South America, the Caribbean, and North America. The contradiction here is that most countries involved in the transatlantic slave trade had laws in their countries forbidding slavery, while outside of their borders, they practiced the slave trade on a large scale.

Can you imagine that at home you forbid your children to kill someone, but as soon as you step outside your home and visit your neighborhood, you start killing on a large scale? What kind of mind can reconcile such a duality? What kind of unhealthy mind is obliged to a law that prohibits a malicious action in his own home but practices what is against the same law somewhere else for personal gain?

The behavior intrigues me. It is the question that lies underneath my exploration of the impact of traumatic events on the mind and body. Most human beings experience at least one traumatic event in their lives. I have experienced one traumatic event in my life as a child when I witnessed my father slapping my mother. This one event had a major impact on my thoughts, emotions, and behavior for at least three decades. I was not able to talk to my father. I was not able to visit him during my vacations on the island. I blamed him as the one responsible for the divorce of my parents. I felt unconsciously jealous of friends who lived in their homes with both parents.

This little event, as you can see, became a big event in my mind. It shaped my views, feelings, and emotions toward my father in an instant. Imagine the impact major events like the ones on this list have had on millions of lives. Imagine the impact of all the habits, thoughts, and actions as a consequence of these traumatic events without the awareness of their existence and origin. Having experienced or witnessed a traumatic event definitely affects our lives. Not being aware of the impact (being unconscious) or ignoring the impact on our thoughts, emotions, and behavior (being conscious but having shame to talk about it) deeply influences our daily lives, relationships, and ultimately our societies. Individual traumas can affect a person's mental health, but intergenerational trauma can affect the collective mental health of future generations and nations.

TRAUMATIC EVENTS

In the book *The Body Keeps the Score: Brain, Mind and Body in the Healing of Trauma,* Dutch psychiatrist Bessel van der Kolk argues that the wide-ranging effects of trauma are experienced not only by traumatized individuals, but also by those around them. Trauma is a collective experience, and it is intergenerational.

Several events in human history stand out as particularly traumatic due to their widespread impact and the suffering they caused. I include on that list:

- **The Black Death (1347–1351).** This pandemic killed an estimated 75–200 million people in Eurasia, wiping out about a third of Europe's population and causing profound social and economic upheaval.
- **The Transatlantic Slave Trade (16th–19th centuries).** The exact number of enslaved Africans transported during the transatlantic slave trade is difficult to determine with absolute certainty due to incomplete records, lost documents, and variations in historical estimates. However, most scholars estimate that between twelve million and 12.8 million Africans were forcibly taken across the Atlantic between the 16th and 19th centuries. The Africans were forcibly transported to the Americas under brutal conditions, suffering immense cruelty and death.
- **World War I (1914–1918).** Known as the Great War, it caused approximately sixteen million deaths and introduced unprecedented levels of destruction and suffering due to trench warfare and chemical weapons.
- **World War II (1939–1945).** This global conflict involved most of the world's nations and resulted in an estimated seventy to eighty-five million deaths, including the Holocaust, where six million Jews were systematically murdered.
- **The Holocaust (1941–1945).** A genocide during World War II, where six million Jews and millions of other minorities were exterminated by the Nazi regime.

- **The Hiroshima and Nagasaki Atomic Bombings (1945).** The United States dropped atomic bombs on these Japanese cities, causing immediate and long-term devastation with over 200,000 deaths.
- **The Great Chinese Famine (1959–1961).** Resulting from a combination of social, political, and natural factors, this famine caused the deaths of an estimated fifteen to forty-five million people.
- **The Rwandan Genocide (1994).** In approximately one hundred days, ethnic Hutu extremists killed about 800,000 Tutsis and moderate Hutus in a brutal campaign of mass murder.
- **September 11 Attacks (2001).** A series of coordinated terrorist attacks by al-Qaeda on the United States resulted in nearly 3,000 deaths and significant global repercussions.
- **The COVID-19 pandemic (2020–2023).** A novel coronavirus that originated in China killed approximately seven million people globally.

Each of these events had profound and lasting effects on the societies involved, shaping the course of history and leaving deep scars on human consciousness.

Trauma isn't just something faced by war veterans—it's far more prevalent in our society than we realize. The truth is that trauma can happen to anyone, and it's time we found out what this really means. Traumas result from an experience of extreme stress or pain that leaves an individual feeling helpless, or too overwhelmed to cope with adversity. Experiences involving war typically result in traumas, but violent crimes and accidents cause them too. Rape and child abuse are terrible events, and they are also unfortunately more common than you might think. Reports reveal that twelve million women were victims of rape in the United States in 2014 alone, and that more than 50 percent of those women were under the age of fifteen at the time of the assault. Every year in the United States, there are three million cases of child abuse. These traumatic experiences can change the lives of those affected, as well as the lives of their friends and family.

THE SCIENCE BEHIND TRAUMA

The Body Keeps the Score explains the science behind the unknown behavior and consequences of traumatic events on our daily lives. If we were aware of our traumas, why we behave as we behave, why we respond the way we respond when something unexpected happens that is deeply stored in our memory and our energy field as a traumatic event, we would have a much healthier mind, much healthier societies, and much healthier nations.

Traumatic experiences leave traces, whether on a large scale (on our histories and cultures) or close to home—on our families—with dark secrets imperceptibly passed down through generations. Traumatic experiences also leave traces on our minds and emotions, on our capacity for joy and intimacy, and even on our biology and immune system. While all human beings want to move beyond trauma, the part of our brain that is devoted to ensuring our survival (deep below our rational brain, which is called the reptilian brain) is not very good at denial, long after a traumatic experience is over. In my personal life, I could not face my father for decades.

A trauma may be reactivated at the slightest hint of danger, mobilize disturbed brain circuits, and secrete massive amounts of stress hormones, adrenaline, or cortisol, and activate the fight-or-flight response. Can you imagine living your whole life unconsciously in this mode, primarily for survival? It will affect your biology and immune system. In my case, even before I studied in the Netherlands, I felt uncomfortable whenever my uncles on my mother's side mentioned my father's name. It would draw up vivid memories of that specific night when he slapped my mother—this would be activated instantly whenever his name was mentioned. I deeply felt the injustice done to my mother and, unconsciously, anger toward my father. At the same time, I felt pain for not having my father in my life during my teen years. I was embarrassed by him and could not face him or talk to him. I was moving away from him. I was in flight mode, not because of an imminent danger or because I was being attacked by a lion. I felt danger toward my own father, someone who used to be my best teacher in everything nature had to offer mankind.

The most important job of the brain is to ensure our survival, even under the most miserable conditions. Everything else is secondary. To do that, brains need to:

- Generate internal signals that register what our bodies need, such as food, rest, protection, sex, and shelter.
- Create a map of the world that points us to where to go to satisfy those needs.
- Generate the energy and actions we need to get us there.
- Warn us of dangers and opportunities along the way.
- Adjust our actions based on the requirements of the moment.

If something happens to the map of the world, which points us where we have to go because of trauma, we will live a life based on a false reality of a wrongly mapped world. All the other steps—generating energy, warning us of danger, and adjusting our actions will be based on the false map created from the traumatic experience.

Because we human beings are mammals, creatures who can only survive and thrive in groups, all these imperatives require coordination and collaboration. What happens when (1) our internal signals don't work, (2) our maps don't lead us where we need to go, (3) we are too paralyzed to move, (4) our actions do not correspond to our needs, or when our relationships break down? Imagine you are walking across the busiest street in New York City, and your internal signals don't register that a car is coming at you at high speed. When you finally see that the car is going to hit you, instead of fleeing to save your life, you become paralyzed. This could actually kill you— that's why the survival mode of our brain is so important. On the other hand, if we constantly live with a map of our life that does not lead us where we need to go, our actions do not correspond to our needs, or we are constantly in broken relationships. This brings us a lot of stress and sadness, a life without joy, a life without the light all human beings have within, a birth gift, and we will live a miserable life.

Psychological problems occur when our internal signals don't work, when our maps don't lead us where we need to go, when we are too paralyzed to move (we could actually get killed), when our actions do not correspond to our needs, or when our relationships break down. Trauma can interfere with all five brain functions.

Research provides the scientific basis for the mind, brain, and body, as well as the impact of trauma on all three. *The Body Keeps the Score* is a simple but powerful teaching about the mind, brain, and body in the transformation of trauma. One of Van der Kolk's teachings that stands out to me is that mindfulness and supportive relationships support trauma recovery. During my presentation of *Healthy Minds—Healthy Nation* at the seminar Prevent Now of ENNIA in October 2016, I presented the result of a Harvard Medical School study about what research tells us about happiness.[2] The primary conclusions:

- We have to value love above everything else.
- Meaningful relationships and connections matter a lot.
- More money and power do not mean more happiness.

Traumatic experiences, as described in *The Body Keeps the Score*, affect the basic functions of our brains in ways that, if left unaddressed, can carry on these effects for a lifetime, from generation to generation, probably resulting in a long-term illness, unhealthy minds, and ultimately unhealthy societies. A malfunction in the basic functions of the brain significantly impacts the actions and behavior of human beings. It is imperative to identify and provide healing practices for a traumatized person to restore and reset the basic functions of the brain so the disequilibrium in the body disappears, healing can manifest, and every human being can show their true spiritual essence, which is

---

2   Harvard Medical School, *Stress Management: Approaches for Preventing and Reducing Stress*, Harvard Medical School Special Health Reports (Harvard Health Publications, 2013).

love. Humanity has been widely focused on Western healing practices based on science, while we have forgotten ancient healing practices based on wisdom. As the shamans of South America say, "Information is knowing that water is H_2O—wisdom is being able to make it rain."

POST-TRAUMATIC STRESS DISORDER

Traumatized people often suffer from post-traumatic stress disorder (PTSD), which can lead to depression and substance abuse. In addition, traumatized people tend to mistrust anyone who hasn't experienced the same suffering they have and assume that nobody can understand them. This was illustrated in one of the therapy groups that van der Kolk set up for Vietnam veterans. While the group helped the veterans find friends and share their experiences, those who weren't traumatized by the war were considered outsiders by the group—including van der Kolk. It took weeks of listening, empathizing, and building trust with the veterans before they accepted him. Establishing a rapport with someone suffering from PTSD is a challenge on its own, so just imagine trying to maintain a marriage, a close friendship, or a stable parent-child relationship. Traumatized people find it difficult to trust even those who love them most, including partners and kids. This can be very tough on friends and families, often leading to estrangement or divorce. When I read this, it made sense to me that the society of Curaçao still experiences contemporary effects of trauma due to the slavery period.

Those who have suffered trauma often experience flashbacks in which they relive the mental and physical experience. Do you ever remember something embarrassing you did and feel yourself squirm or blush? Then you've got a tiny insight into how memories of trauma can impact the body. When PTSD sufferers are reminded of their trauma, their body and brain enter a high-stress mode, because they experience the memory as if it were real. This is called a flashback, an impact of trauma the author studied in an experiment van der Kolk carried out with his patients.

The negative impacts of childhood trauma can carry over into adulthood, van der Kolk writes. Traumatic experiences are hard enough to deal with as an adult, but there is nothing more difficult than facing trauma as a young child. With brains that aren't even fully developed, children who undergo trauma are at greater risk of experiencing a wide range of negative consequences. These consequences surface in the years immediately following their experiences and later in adulthood.

Traumatized children often expect bad things to happen. Van der Kolk demonstrated this in an experiment in which cards with pictures from magazines were shown to children who had experienced trauma and to those who hadn't. The goal of the experiment was to examine how trauma affects perception and memory. The findings showed that traumatized children often misinterpreted neutral or ambiguous images as threatening or dangerous. For example, when shown a picture of a person with a neutral or slightly surprised expression, the traumatized children were more likely to interpret the face as angry or hostile. In contrast, children without trauma history were more likely to interpret the images in a neutral or benign way.

This is a valid explanation for the lack of collaboration, rooted in envy, that still prevails in Curaçao's society today. Father and mother slaves that have experienced traumatic events in their childhood will live their lives based on these experiences and pass this life story to the next generations. Father and mother slaves from cattle slavery who have been programmed deliberately for rule and division to weaken the collective force, intrinsically have the feeling of jealousy and envy when someone else is being promoted. Promotion during slavery means better conditions for your life. This envy has been unconsciously passed from generation to generation. We can still experience this behavior today, not only in Curaçao but everywhere in the Caribbean, descendants of transatlantic slavery. It's time to become conscious, it's time to start the healing process, and it is time to tap into your light within.

While normal memories fade and change, traumatic memories are vivid, unchanging, and easily triggered. When we tell stories, we tend to embellish, exaggerate, or omit parts of our experiences. By the fifth time you've told a story, chances are it'll be quite different from the first version. We even remember things differently over time. Why is this?

In general, we don't memorize the sensory details of events. Most of us remember what we did or how we felt in general, but we don't store vivid memories about the smell of the room we were in or the exact details of someone's face. But it's a different story when it comes to traumatic memories—we remember these situations vividly, and the memories don't change over time.

HEALING FROM TRAUMA

While trauma presents a number of challenges, there are ways to heal. Let's discuss those now.

EMDR, eye movement desensitization and reprocessing, is an effective therapy technique that helps patients integrate their memories and restore a sense of agency over their mind and body. It may sound simple, in that it involves the therapist holding up one finger and moving it back and forth across a patient's field of vision. While the patient follows the finger with their eyes, they are guided through a traumatic memory and encouraged to make new associations.

Yoga offers trauma sufferers a safe way to explore the relationship between their body and mind. Our body and mind share a close relationship. To live a balanced, stable life, we need to understand how our emotions work, and how they impact our bodies. Unfortunately, trauma can make this challenging. Trauma often leaves people with a hypersensitive alarm system (fight or flight) in their bodies. Those who suffered sexual abuse as children, for example, discover they experience crippling panic in harmless situations, such as cuddling with their partner.

Yoga is an ancient practice focusing on breathing, flexibility, and strength to boost mental well-being. It comprises a set of physical, mental, and spiritual practices or disciplines. The main components of yoga are breathing and postures (a series of movements designed to increase strength and flexibility). The practice is said to have originated more than five thousand years ago in India and has been adopted in other countries in various ways. This is an excellent example of how an ancient practice is suggested as a healing alternative for trauma based on scientific research.

Mindfulness and supportive relationships are essential to trauma recovery. Mindfulness is a trendy concept right now, but it's not just a fad—it's an incredibly effective lifestyle choice. It also constitutes a powerful tool for trauma recovery, but how does it work?

Mindfulness is about maintaining a conscious awareness of your body and your emotions, rather than denying them. This is especially tough after trauma, as painful memories cause us to repress our emotions rather than address them. Mindfulness is one of the many meditation techniques—there is also activity meditation and transcendental meditation. Ahead, in part IV of the book, we'll go deeper into the ancient wisdoms of transcendental meditation and shamanism, the how, and the why.

Neurofeedback helps trauma sufferers rewire their brains. Did you know that electrical signals are responsible for just about everything that goes on in your brain? These brain waves govern our thought processes, so they're quite important. Unfortunately, they can also be damaged by trauma. Let's find out how. There are many different types of brain waves, including alpha waves, which are triggered when we feel calm and relaxed. A recent study at the University of Adelaide in Australia examined soldiers who served in Iraq or Afghanistan and found that the longer they spent in the war zone, the fewer alpha waves their brains produced. Instead, soldiers produced brain waves similar to those of children diagnosed with ADHD, hampering their ability to relax, stay calm, and focus.

Mindfulness practices are tremendously effective for trauma recovery, and van der Kolk emphasizes this in his book. Transcendental meditation teaches us how to cultivate a healthy and calm mind daily. As said by the Roman Emperor Marcus Aurelius, "The nearer a man comes to a calm mind, the closer he is to strength." From my personal experience, I understand that Marcus Aurelius meant a calm mind is a mind free of fear, free of anger, free of trauma, free of greed, and free of envy. By "closer to his strength," I believe Marcus Aurelius means we are closer to the inner light, closer to our soul purpose, closer to serving humanity with love and abundance instead of fear, anger, trauma, greed, and envy.

Shamanism teaches us the science of our luminous energy fields, which consist of our chakras. The practices teach us how to turn wounds into sources of wisdom and compassion, as I had to learn to turn my wound toward my father into compassion to forgive him. Shamanism teaches us to reset the fight-or-flight system to feel safe in the world and our daily lives. Shamanism teaches us how to illuminate our luminous energy field. It teaches the extraction process, which removes intrusive energies from our luminous energy field. Shamanism teaches us tracking skills to trace energy lines into the past, in this life, or even past lives, to identify if a soul was separated from its core purpose due to a traumatic event. It reveals how to recover the original contract of the soul through soul retrieval. Shamanism teaches us about the great death rites—how to die consciously so we can live a life without fear and die fearlessly.

In upcoming chapters, I will provide a detailed explanation about the ancient teachings of transcendental meditation and shamanism. I will share my personal journey based on the traumas I have experienced. Remember, suffering is not a punishment, it's a choice—it's a wake-up call to tap into the light within. It's a call **to wake up**: to awaken our spiritual growth; **to grow up**: to grow spiritually and strengthen our light within; and **to show up**: to actually do something about unconscious behavior because we are all living in the soup, and unconsciousness is all around us.

Part III

Beginning to Awaken

CHAPTER 10

The Golden Cage

My journey of awakening was set in motion by a particularly difficult professional and legal ordeal I went through after moving back to Curaçao in 2003 and taking a job at a company named ENNIA. In this chapter, I will chronicle how it all went down and how it sparked my awakening. As you look ahead to your awakening journey, I hope you will draw comfort from the story and know that you are not alone in your pain. You will likely recognize from your challenging life experiences the excruciating tenor of this pain (not just emotional but physical) I endured, the sleepless nights I spent staring at the ceiling. On a more positive note, however, you will see how—and draw comfort from—it was those very same terrible experiences that inspired me to search for answers to alleviate my pain and calm my mind. Ultimately, the ENNIA saga also taught me the importance of speaking up. This too will become an essential tool as you move forward with your mission of healing your mind and nation.

As for me, it all began with my move back to Curacao. After fifteen years living in the Netherlands, everything in me longed to return to the homeland that had shaped my early life. My mission to study and gain sufficient, relevant work experience was done, and it was time to leave. I did not succeed in becoming a doctor, nor did I succeed in securing work as a chemical engineer, but I was not disappointed. I simply trusted that it was not meant for me to become a doctor or chemical engineer.

So I left my job at Delta Lloyd in the Netherlands in 2003 and took a job that brought me to Curaçao as a managing director of one of Delta Lloyd's full subsidiaries, a company named ENNIA. I left for ENNIA's Amerfoortse Antillen with a return guarantee to Delta Lloyd, one of the largest insurance companies in the Netherlands at that time. The Group Human Resources Director assured me I could return anytime within three years. ENNIA had just bought Amerfoortse and Onderlinge Hulp from ASR Insurances in Rotterdam, which, by acquiring Amerfoortse Antillen, gave ENNIA the largest health insurance portfolio in the Netherlands Antilles. It was not a profitable portfolio.

My job was to uphold the strategic objectives of ENNIA: One, to integrate these two portfolios into one. Two, to make sure the total portfolio was profitable within three years. And three, erase the name Amerfoortse Antillen from the local market. I was very excited about the new challenge. I set myself up to execute these objectives: One, convert the products of Amertfoortse to the ENNIA system. Two, execute financial intervention to make the combined portfolio profitable. And three, change the label of Amersfoortse Antillen to ENNIA Zorg, which translates as ENNIA Healthcare.

With the acquisition of Amerfoorste, ENNIA Zorg became the largest private health insurance company in the Dutch Antilles— including Curaçao, Aruba, Bonaire, St. Maarten, St. Eustatius, and Saba—with a portfolio of almost 17,000 policies. Health insurance is key to a nation's objective of achieving a healthy nation from a curative perspective. However, it is known that the margins for health insurance are small, which means, efficiency of each health insurance portfolio and claims management are key to profitability. Claim percentage normally varies between 75 percent and 80 percent, which leaves only 25 percent to 20 percent for the other operational costs and a small profit margin. A healthcare insurance company that is not profitable, even with a small margin, is not sustainable and may lead to the decision to stop selling health insurance policies. So it would be my mission to make this work.

One innovation I spearheaded to make this a tight operation was the Medicard, an identification card with the name of the insurer, date of birth, type of insurance (individual or collective), type of product, and details of the insurer's insurance coverage. On the other side of the Medicard is the healthcare provider for the insured. This gave the insured a sense of security—"I am insured"—and allowed them to receive healthcare without having to pay up front (and then get reimbursed). From our standpoint, it made the processing of claims more efficient.

By 2004—2005, the transition from Amersfoortse to ENNIA Zorg was complete. But then a new development was brewing. Delta Lloyd was moving to sell off ENNIA. And this is when the trouble began. At the time, I did not view the decision to sell ENNIA as a risk to me—it could even be an opportunity as long as the buyer was a candidate with an in-depth, proven insurance track record and the attention and presence for the region—the Caribbean and Latin America. Two suitors quickly rose to the top of the list: Parman International from Hushang Ansary, an Iranian American company, and Multinational de Seguros from Tobias Carrero from Venezuela. Both possibilities were bound to change the corporate culture.

ENNIA culture had been characterized by deep and solid insurance knowledge. Multinational Insurance was a multinational insurance company that had built its presence in Venezuela, Panama, and Puerto Rico. At the time, we knew very little about Parman International, which turned out to be the winner. The acquisition went through in February 2005, but it was indirect. In December 2004, Parman bought Banco di Caribe, one of the largest banks in Curaçao, and Banco di Caribe bought ENNIA in February 2005.

With all these changes, I eventually ended up with a new CEO—Gijsbert van Doorn, who, after reviewing my performance with the integration of the healthcare portfolios and the objective to make the combined portfolio profitable, asked me to be his Chief Operation Officer in 2006. The new governance structure shifted from a product-oriented company (general insurance and life insurance) to a more client-oriented company (front office and back office). The product-oriented structure was a traditional structure for most insurance companies. The client-oriented structure was necessary to serve the client more appropriately.

A new shareholder, Hushang Ansary, visited the ENNIA offices shortly after acquiring the company in 2006. In his address to all employees, he explained that:

- Banco di Caribe and ENNIA should become a solid financial conglomerate: banking and insurance.
- Children of employees of the companies should have access to affordable scholarships to study in the United States.
- Parman International will build affordable houses for the middle and lower classes of Curaçao.

These promises were received with great enthusiasm by all employees. But soon there would be signs of trouble.

Shortly after the acquisition of ENNIA in February 2006, Ansary installed an investment committee and appointed himself as the chairman. He ordered an investment of millions in an affiliated company, transferring millions from ENNIA Life to this affiliated company, which from a governance point of view is a conflict of interest. The former investment manager of ENNIA resigned immediately because of this action. This should have been seen as the first sign of trouble. I was at that time a managing director of Amserfoortse, which became ENNIA Zorg, and was finalizing the aftercare points of the conversion, integration, and name change. I had not become COO in the new corporate structure yet.

Management of the assets and investments of a life insurance company is the direct responsibility of the management of the board of directors of the company. There should be an asset liability management plan that matches the obligations of the liabilities—short, mid-, and long term—and the required return of the assets to match the obligations of the liabilities. However, it would soon become clear that Ansary had a totally different view of how to manage an insurance company. Premiums were seen as the shareholders' money—not as they should be, where premiums are paid by insurers and entrusted to the company. Assets and provisions for pension insurance were invested in affiliated companies of the shareholder, not held in compliance and maintained for solvency. For pension insurance, which is a long-term obligation, the solvency of the insurer is of great importance. Solvency, in finance or business, is the degree to which the current assets of the insurance company or entity exceed the current liabilities of that individual or entity. In simple terms, does the insurance company generate enough return with the assets to cover the obligations of the liabilities now, but also ten, twenty, and thirty years in the future? To do this you need liquidity (cash, and cash is king) and you need solvency, which protects your long-term obligations. (The obligations in this case are the monthly pension payments of every insurer from the moment that person reaches the pension age until the moment that person dies, which could be ten, twenty, or thirty years ahead.)

As the chief operations officer, I was responsible for making sure these payments were protected because it was key to keeping the clients' trust. The insurance business is built on trust. I, as a client, trust that by paying the premiums according to the policy conditions, the insurance company in return will keep the promise for claims payment in case of non-life insurance due to an unforeseen event (accident, illness, or hurricane) or in case future payments in case of life insurance due to a pension, which is kind of a life annuity.

Over the course of five years, from 2006 up to 2011, Ansary took a series of actions that jeopardized the solvency of the life insurance arm, ENNIA Life. By 2021, these actions would be documented in a report by an external actuarial company, which would be presented to the court in Curaçao. In short, the report documented eight violations.

MY BODY AND MIND ARE ON CONSTANT ALERT

My experience of chronic lower-back pain originated in 2004, just one year after I returned to Curaçao. I had three surgeries—in 2005, 2007, and 2011—to address the issue. During these seven years, I experienced a constant level of "unpleasant and uncomfortable"—nothing could bring relief, including exercise, painkillers, and swimming. I tried everything. At a certain moment, I could not even work for many days. I would have to take a break at noon and come home and use a hot pack on my lower back to ease the pain.

From the moment the new shareholder from Parman International took over the company in 2006 until the day I resigned at ENNIA in 2017, my body and mind had been on constant alert. From the moment I noticed the impropriety of handling funds, I was in peril.

Let me explain why Ansary and others' actions were not prudent. It is common knowledge in investing that you should not invest all your eggs in one basket. From a risk perspective, your investments should be spread out. For the life insurance arm of ENNIA, at a certain moment in 2009/2010, I saw that 85 percent of the assets were in two baskets—and both eggs were owned by the shareholder. A prudent cut-off margin for life insurance is considered to be a maximum of 15 percent to 20 percent of investments in the same basket.

I could see this would be quite a battle. I was the whistleblower. I was on the opposing side, and, at a certain moment, I became a threat to them, and I had to leave. During this time, it became quite a challenge to balance maintaining my integrity with that of the company, which held the trust of the policyholders. The stress affected my peace of mind. I could not sleep well at night because I kept asking myself how the shareholder would solve this solvency gap.

That was the main reason I started meditating, and it brought immediate relief. I found a local transcendental meditation teacher, and we met in a room on the second floor of a building in the neighborhood of Scharloo. As soon as I began, the activities of my mind started to calm down. I could sense stillness and tranquility. I tapped into the light for the first time. I wanted to know everything about this internal sanctuary.

Looking back now, it's clear that the succession of surgeries was undoubtedly the consequence of being in an environment that my true self (my soul) knew was not my home. I did not know that back then, but I know it now. What happens when life squeezes us? What happens when we experience suffering? These experiences can be gifts that help us identify areas we need to improve.

Through the years, I have found that transcendental meditation and shamanism (wake-up phase and grow-up phase) have helped me grow spiritually and understand the cause and origin of pain. In my case, the L5 vertebra is the lowest one, and it articulates with the sacrum, affecting my flexibility and relationship with time on Earth. Genetic history and ancestral lineage play a significant role in how one navigates life with or without the support of family. Emotional distress can arise when individuals feel out of place. This pain is often associated with a sense of not being rooted in one's environment. You may feel like you do not fit in with your family, that they don't understand you, or you haven't found your tribe—the people who truly accept and comprehend you.

ENNIA was not my tribe. ENNIA was not my home. Whenever there was a board meeting at a luxurious hotel, and we had to travel by private jets, I felt a sense of injustice. I did not feel comfortable at all and participated in just a few of them. I realized I was living in a "golden cage," meaning I was somewhere, doing something that did not meet my true purpose on this earth. Not only was it a golden cage, but it was the contradiction of fighting for a higher purpose—for the clients, for myself—because I'm also a pension client, my family, for Curaçao. Underneath this, I risked having to leave Curaçao and return to the Netherlands, which meant uprooting myself and my family. It became a battle between staying in my homeland versus guarding my integrity and peace of mind. No wonder I was not sleeping at night.

I say that I faced having to leave Curaçao because ENNIA offered one of the best employment options on Curaçao. ENNIA was innovative. Because of my work, ENNIA had become the first insurance company in Curaçao to issue a Medicard. It also became the first insurance company for general insurances, starting with online sales of travel insurance, a campaign that proved to be a huge success. Gross premiums for travel insurance increased from $82,417, when we started in 2012 to $1,044,000 when I left. I was very proud of the progress that ENNIA made despite all the challenges—proud to be the first, proud to innovate in a saturated insurance market, proud to grow and increase the premiums for non-life insurance premiums in that market.

During that period, ENNIA had one of the best commercial campaigns in the history of the company called "Imagine It All Gone," which aimed to increase awareness about why it was important to have insurance. "Imagine you will lose your luggage during your vacation, and you do not have travel insurance," was one of the lines in the campaign. I was promoted to senior managing director in 2011 based on my knowledge of insurance, which gave me seniority as a managing director, but more importantly, someone who made things happen.

I was climbing the ladder, which was not the main objective, although I said before starting my employment at ENNIA, that one day I would like to be the CEO of ENNIA. But climbing the ladder and having success was also taking its toll. A managing director must safeguard the objectives of the company by all means, and climbing the ladder meant I would be closer to the shareholders, including the one who would accuse me of impropriety. I thought that together with the new CEO who promoted me in 2011, we could change course and convince Ansary to address the solvency deficit of ENNIA Life Insurances. I was convinced it could be done, and that's the main reason I have stayed so long at ENNIA. I am a fighter. Whenever there is injustice, I do not walk away. I try to correct the injustice just as my mother did.

Together with other managing directors and key management team members, we addressed the solvency deficit, and presented solutions to the shareholders, the board of supervisors, directors, and the Central Bank of Curaçao and St. Maarten. Most of the managing directors had left ENNIA. They were expats, and it was easy to quit and leave the island. For me, it was difficult, not because I could not find another job, but because I had an excellent job offer from one of the largest banks in 2008. For me, it was difficult because I was from the island, and employees and clients trusted me. They trusted that, although we had challenges, we would find a solution for the shortcomings. This is both an advantage and a liability; an advantage to be trusted and a liability to become liable for the shortcomings of ENNIA Life. I took my pledge seriously. Here is a line from the company manual: "A director is fully liable for mismanagement unless he cannot be blamed seriously and he has not been negligent in taking measures to avert the consequences of the mismanagement."

This is key. It outlined my risk of staying too long at ENNIA. If I had remained silent, or if I had not been successful in getting us back into compliance, then I would have risked becoming liable. I knew I could prove that I had not been negligent in taking measures to avert the consequences of the mismanagement to invest the assets of ENNIA Life in affiliated companies (assets) of the shareholder, but I didn't like being this close to the fire.

I stayed for as long as I could to convince all the stakeholders—the shareholders, my colleagues who were managing directors, and the regulatory entities—to address the solvency deficit. It felt like a moral obligation to solve the shortcoming; I'm not a quitter—I'm a fighter.

I know you are too.

CHAPTER 11

What's Love Got to Do with It?

Love may seem like a strange subject for a book about healing the mind. But here's the thing: it is very hard to achieve the kind of awakening you crave if you are in a marriage or relationship with someone who is not on the same path or has the same awareness. That's what happened to me. But the opposite is also true. Loving someone you're truly aligned with can help to facilitate your own awakening.

That's definitely what my second wife, my queen Chantal, has done for me. It all started decades ago, and I wasn't even aware of it. The first time Chantal was in my presence, I didn't remember her. We still laugh and make jokes about that moment. It was at the graduation of her older sister, Daisy Seferina, who studied civil engineering at the Technical University of Delft in the Netherlands. I had become friends with Daisy, and she invited me to her graduation in October 1999. I went there with my life partner, Sandra, who was the mother of our son, Jairzinho. Sandra and I were not married yet. The graduation party was a nice ceremony, and there is a picture of Daisy, her friends, Sandra, and me. The one who took the picture was Chantal.

She still teases me that my eyes were clouded. After that day, I didn't
see Chantal until 2010, eleven years later, when her name appeared
to me again.

It was in May 2010, and I was working at ENNIA as COO. That
year the FRED Foundation was hosting Career Organization Days at
a career fair in the World Trade Centrum of Rotterdam, Netherlands.
ENNIA needed key functions to streamline its services to clients—one
of which was a customer service manager. When ENNIA posted all
the vacancies, FRED matched the vacancies with potential candidates.
That's how I received Chantal's resume, and it was very impressive. She
had graduated cum laude from the Technical University of Delft, where
she had studied Technical Administrative Science. She was working
at the largest bank of the Netherlands, ABN AMRO, as manager of
retail banking at two different locations: Amsterdam and Eindhoven.
I immediately scheduled an interview with her. The human resource
manager and I were blown away. Chantal was energetic, enthusiastic,
values-driven, positive, highly intelligent, and highly disciplined.

We both concluded that Chantal would be the perfect candidate to
serve as ENNIA's customer service manager. It was a new department,
so I knew its implementation had to be militarized with the proper
change management competencies, and Chantal definitely had them.
We made her an offer.

At the time, Chantal was married, and they had two children: a
daughter, Aimee, and a son, Antoine. Chantal emigrated from the
Netherlands to Curaçao in November 2010, and she started to work
for ENNIA in December 2010. Her presence within ENNIA was felt
immediately. Her positivism, energy, and discipline have infused
ENNIA and the new customer service department highly. Two years
in, she won the ENNIA employee of the year award, an award well-
deserved. Chantal became one of my best recruitments for ENNIA
at the job fairs in the Netherlands. She reported to me, and we developed mutual respect. Together with an enthusiastic ENNIA team,
we implemented significant positive changes that improved client
services; streamlined the customer experience for life and non-life

insurance; and we developed competitive products for vehicle and property insurances.

As Om Shanti expresses in Sanskrit, "The universe puts you in touch with people and situations that have the same vibration. The higher your vibration, the more miracles will happen for you and the world." This was what was happening with my queen, Chantal, and me. We had the same energy levels. We started fast out of the gate with seminars at ENNIA to make great things happen for ENNIA and the inhabitants of Curaçao.

This led me to present "Healthy Minds—Healthy Nation," a seminar talk in which I described the importance of a healthy nation from the perspective of an insurance company. At that time, I could never have known that it would become the title of my first book. My spiritual transformation started right there. This was still when I thought ENNIA could become an enlightened company.

Although the situation at ENNIA deteriorated in 2012/2013 when the Central Bank of Curaçao and St. Maarten announced that valuation guidelines for life insurance companies would change, the dark clouds started to gather with media attention on July 1, 2016. The renowned Dutch newspaper FD (Financial Newspaper) published a front-page article about ENNIA with the headline, "Insurance company ENNIA drained under the eyes of the Central Bank." The article spurred a series of questions from clients and rocked their trusts. As a senior managing director, I made many presentations to key clients to explain exactly what happened.

By this time, Chantal was the managing director who joined me for all these presentations—I had been promoted, and then she was promoted to my previous position. I was in a relationship that ended at the beginning of 2016, when things got worse at ENNIA. On a business trip to St. Maarten in the autumn of 2016, there was a seminar about the added value of insurance companies. I suddenly saw Chantal in a new way. Our plane departed from St. Maarten for the flight to Curaçao, and after fifteen minutes, we experienced severe turbulence.

Chantal, who was sitting next to me, grabbed my hand. I looked her in the eyes, and then I asked, "Can you handle it?"

She looked at me solidly and answered, "Yes, I can."

After all these years, I know now for sure that my question to her, "Can you handle it?" was not only about the turbulence on the plane but also turbulence in our lives. From the moment she said, "Yes, I can," I saw her not only as my colleague, or even as a *"ruman"* (which means brother/sister), as we were calling each other, but as a beautiful, intelligent woman.

That same year, her relationship with her husband was deteriorating, leading to a separation in the first quarter of 2017. The day I quit my job at ENNIA, Chantal was still working there, and two managing directors asked her if she wanted to be promoted to the job I had just left. She declined, and she quit her job at ENNIA in July 2017, one month after my resignation. Since both of us were without jobs, we spent quite some time talking on the phone about our experience at ENNIA, sharing how we actually saw life. We shared about the values and norms most important to us, which were exactly the same, perhaps because our parents provided similar sets of values.

One noteworthy event was a group picture for the 2016 annual report. The photographer who took that picture in the ENNIA office in Otrabanda, after reviewing several positions of the managing directors of ENNIA, requested Chantal and me to be in the front of the picture, saying, "You give life and color to the picture."

After the photographer took the picture, she asked us, "Gilbert, Chantal, are you married?"

I answered, "No, we are not; we are colleagues."

She said, "Well, you look like a couple."

Apparently, she saw something in us that we did not yet see at that time.

Figure 5: Picture at the ENNIA office in Otrabanda

In autumn 2017, after both of us left ENNIA, she ended her marriage. We became really close, and our friendship, built on trust and shared values through great turbulence, began to blossom into a relationship based on mutual respect, honesty, and appreciation. I started to see Chantal as my partner, my wife, my queen, and I have never stopped seeing her that way. Together we have five children—she has three children from her first marriage: Aimee, Antoine, and Angele. I have two children from my first marriage: Jairzinho and Jorzinho.

Figure 6: Vacation at Amerongse Berg, Netherlands in July 2024

Our unconditional love for each other is special. "The measure of love is to love without measure," a writing often attributed to St. Augustine of Hippo. In the summer of 2019, we took a vacation to Toronto, Niagara Falls, and Montreal in Canada. I saw Niagara Falls as the perfect place to propose to Chantal. Before the vacation, I arranged for a professional photographer in Canada to immortalize the moment of our engagement. After breakfast one morning, as the taxi dropped us off at Niagara Falls, I informed our children Jorzinho, Aimee, Antoine, and Angele that I was going to propose to Chantal and assigned each a task. Aimee and Angele would carry the engagement ring. Jairzinho and Antoine were in charge of the music (Jairzinho could not accompany us during that vacation). I had chosen Ed Sheeran's song, "Thinking Out Loud," to play when the moment came that I would kneel before her. That morning, everyone played their roles perfectly.

After the first group picture at Niagara Falls, I said, "Let's go to a small park close by to take more pictures."

When we got to the park, I got down on one knee. Jairzinho and Antoine played the Ed Sheeran song. Chantal was pleasantly surprised. I wrote a short speech to tell her:

In times of great turbulence, in times of dark clouds, every dark cloud has a silver lining. You have been the silver lining through the turbulent times at ENNIA. I have seen you, and now I will never lose you from my sight. Do you want to marry me?

She said, "I will!"

Surrounded by four of our children, we felt so happy. A tourist bus had stopped, and now they were clapping their hands to congratulate us. It was a beautiful engagement ceremony, close to the powerful energy of Niagara Falls.

Figure 7: Chantal's reaction after proposal in 2019 at Niagara Falls

Figure 8: On my knees for my queen

Figure 9: Happy faces after the proposal ceremony

Figure 10: Group picture after the proposal ceremony

In September of that same year, 2019, we bought a house so we could finally live together. Since 2018, we have been living apart but together. We started dreaming about our wedding—our dream was to marry close to the ocean, just as our engagement was near the powerful Niagara Falls. We decided to set December 12, 2020, as our wedding date. We married on the balcony of our weekend house at Westpunt with an ocean view. It was during the COVID-19 lockdown, and we could invite only a limited number of guests—our parents, brother, sisters, nieces, nephews, and the closest aunties. Our photoshoot before the wedding was on the beach of Playa Piscado at Westpunt, where we took some beautiful pictures.

Figure 11: Wedding picture at Playa Piskadó Westpunt

Chantal became a once-in-a-lifetime person for me. The intelligent, energetic, positive, and highly disciplined young woman who was invisible to me in October 1999 reappeared to me in 2010. It took us twelve years to realize we were destined to be together. In February 2025, we decided to do a DNA ancestry test together, and guess what? Fifty-six percent of her ancestral region comes from Benin & Togo, 11 percent from the Ivory Coast and Ghana for a total of 67 percent of her ancestral region from West Africa, and 66 percent of my ancestral region comes from Benin and Togo, 10 percent from the Ivory Coast, and Ghana for a total of 76 percent of my ancestral region from West Africa. A coincidence, I don't think so. Our families were together long before we could ever dream of being together.

We love each other and the universe!

CHAPTER 12

We Are in the Soup— Unconsciousness Is All Around Us

Part of developing a healthy mind means being able, finally, to discover and act on your true purpose. And when you tap into your purpose, what that really means—in shaman terms—is you are now co-creating with the universe.

After I left ENNIA in June 2017, my intention was to take a break of at least three to four months. I needed a short sabbatical because the last years of my employment at ENNIA had been stressful. During those last years at ENNIA, I had been forced to search for alternative ways to cultivate a calm mind and had started to practice transcendental meditation.

Soon after leaving ENNIA, I ran into the former Prime Minister of Curaçao on a Sunday at Playa Forti's beach in Westpunt. My exit from ENNIA was all over the news, so he asked me what happened. I explained to him the reasons behind my departure from ENNIA. He told me I was completely right and I should not worry because someone with my experience and character will receive plenty of job offers; otherwise, he would be calling me to help the government. The funny thing is that when I left ENNIA, I had only one request to the Great Spirit, or God, as we call the Universe in the Western world. My request was to guide me to the place where I can be of service for the greater interest of Curaçao.

The shamans of the Americas say that when you are in balance with the Universe, you will have total synchronicity and will start co-creating with the Universe. I know I must pay attention to my requests to the Universe because I was blessed with not only one major interest for the island of Curaçao but two: the Refinery and the Hospital.

The prophecy of Pachacutti, rooted in Andean tradition, foretells a great world reversal or upheaval, often described as a "turning over of time and space," in which the established order collapses and a new era of reversal begins. In Inca history, Pachacutti, the ninth Sapa Inca was seen as the ruler who fulfilled this prophecy by transforming the small Cusco kingdom into the vast Inca empire, bringing order from chaos and laying the foundations of Tawantinsuyu. Spiritually, the prophecy symbolizes cycles of destruction and rebirth, teaching that when imbalance, corruption, or disharmony dominate the world, a cosmic shift will occur, restoring balance, justice, and harmony between humans, nature, and the sacred.

I feel like I have been through my own Pachcutti, from the corporate world dominated by power, money, and egos to an awakening to be a guardian of the harmony between humans, nature, and the wisdom from our ancestors.

What about you?

FINDING YOUR PURPOSE THROUGH GNOSIS

Discovering and acting on your purpose in the world we live in nowadays feels like what the Greek philosophers called "gnosis" or "knowing." Knowing transcends rational thought and is often seen as direct, experiential awareness of the truth or the divine. Rather than relying solely on logical proof, spiritual knowledge is about inner illumination (the light within), intuition, and union with a higher reality. Mystical traditions describe it as gnosis, an intimate recognition of the sacred within oneself and the cosmos. This kind of knowledge emphasizes transformation, wisdom, and harmony, suggesting that true knowledge is not just about understanding the world but about becoming aligned with it at the deepest level.

In my personal case, knowing means I was selected to do almost the impossible at the Refinery and the Hospital. I have been threatened, but I never felt alone while climbing these two huge mountains because I knew I had to execute these tasks. I didn't know why back then, but I know it now. The experiences of ENNIA, the Refinery, and the Hospital were all part of my preparation and journey toward writing this book. In the midst of all these experiences, I sometimes felt like a salmon swimming against the current with great force to stop the swim, but I knew it had a greater purpose. Along the way, the purpose gets stronger and clearer.

The call of spirit is unstoppable.

Part IV

Ancestral Healing Wisdom

CHAPTER 13

Transcendental Meditation

I started to have sleepless nights when I learned of the solvency short-age at ENNIA. I was the trusted face of ENNIA. But now I carried the knowledge of all the warnings given to the shareholder, demanding that he take action to correct the matter. It started to take a toll on my health. Now his problem and ENNIA's problem became my problem. I could not sleep properly anymore, with many thoughts about why this had happened and when it would be solved.

My mind was not at peace—that's what triggered me to start look-ing for alternatives so I could have a calm mind even in times of great turbulence. My suffering became a strong motivation. Learning to meditate according to TM was not only quite effective for the sleep-less nights, but it has also increased my curiosity about spirituality. I began a search for spirituality, and the most ancient teachings guided me to shamanism. After I read the book *Shaman, Healer Sage—How to Heal Yourself* and other books by Dr. Alberto Villoldo about the energy medicine of the Americas, I knew instantly that this was the path to follow.

In February 2017, I booked a retreat, "Grow a New Body" at Los Lobos Sanctuary in Chile, Villoldo's home base, and the home of Marcela Lobos. It was life changing—shamanistic work has become part of my daily life since then.

OUR MIND IS AN OCEAN

Our minds can best be compared with an ocean—active at the surface through what we perceive with our five main senses: sight, sound, smell, taste, and touch. If we perceive danger from one of those senses, although in reality there is no danger, it has a great influence on our mind and body. The more information we sense or perceive, the more active our mind will become. It is the same with the surface of the ocean. During a hurricane, the surface of the ocean will be extremely turbulent with massive waves. However, if we dive deep to the bottom of the ocean, it is calm.

The same analogy holds for our minds. When we are active, it is predominantly gamma brain waves (> 38 Hz) that are measured, while during our sleep, it is predominantly delta brain waves (< 4 Hz). Delta and theta brain waves (4–8 Hz) are excellent for healing our mind and body. That's why we feel so relaxed and refreshed after a good night's sleep. Twenty minutes of good meditation can provide the same relaxation effect as a good night's sleep.

As human beings who are essentially spiritual and light beings, we are connected to the universe and everything that consists of energy. Understanding the connection between all living organisms and the universe, or the Great Spirit, can lead to a destiny where we not only create happiness and abundance for ourselves but also for our loved ones, community, country, and the world. Sharing happiness never decreases it. A destiny free of anger, fear, jealousy, greed, and worry is not only desirable but mandatory—we have to create a better world for future generations.

MEDITATION FUNDAMENTALS

How can we as human beings gain a good understanding of the fundamental reality of life that lies in the field of abstract being? How can we become aware that life is not only the body and the mind? How can we become aware that there is a fundamental reality that is our soul (being), and it must be nourished to glorify our lives? Like the tree, we cannot see its roots because they are hidden underground. The soul cannot be perceived with our senses, which are oriented to the external. In the same way, these roots are fundamental for a healthy tree, so is the abstract of being (our soul) necessary for a healthy human life. The roots of the tree provide anchorage and support, absorption of water and nutrients, storage of food and nutrients, the transport of water and nutrients, soil interaction, and ecosystem support. Our soul has the same function—it provides anchorage and support against our ego and all of life's mundane temptations. Our soul is pure energy. Our soul is connected to the whole universe, which can be considered the ecosystem that gives us a sense of "we" instead of "me."

The *Science of Being and the Art of Living* by Maharishi Mahesh Yogi is a foundational text in the Transcendental Meditation (TM) movement, offering a blend of spiritual, philosophical, and practical guidance on achieving personal fulfillment, inner peace, and global harmony. First published in 1963, the book introduces readers to the core principles of TM and explores its benefits for individuals and society. Maharishi's teachings center on the idea that the mind can access a transcendent state, a pure level of consciousness that brings greater harmony, creativity, and purpose to one's life.

Again, transcendental meditation uses the analogy of the ocean to describe our minds. The technique of transcendental meditation helps us turn our focus inward, an inner orientation instead of an external one through our senses. Imagine you are in a small boat in the middle of the Atlantic Ocean and a storm is coming, stirring up huge waves: twenty, thirty, forty-yard high waves. The ocean seems active at the surface with these huge waves, but if we cut a cross-section of the ocean all the way to the deepest level 2.5, 3.1, 4.4 miles deep at the bottom, the ocean is absolutely quiet and calm. Our mind is the same—active at the surface through our senses and what we perceive, and quiet inside, where we experience the source of our thoughts, our true self. We are stuck in the active surface mind due to all the noise and distraction, all the daily activities, all the issues, and all the challenges. We live in an environment where "storms" have become a constant factor. The emergence of social media during the last decades: Facebook, Instagram, LinkedIn, Twitter (X), TikTok, Snapchat, and so on has increased the noise and turbulence at the surface of our minds through our senses. Don't get me wrong, all these platforms are valuable when used properly, but they can be a huge source of distraction. They are a source of information that can become an addiction; only information and data received through our senses govern our daily activities instead of our inner light and inner strength, our true self, our soul.

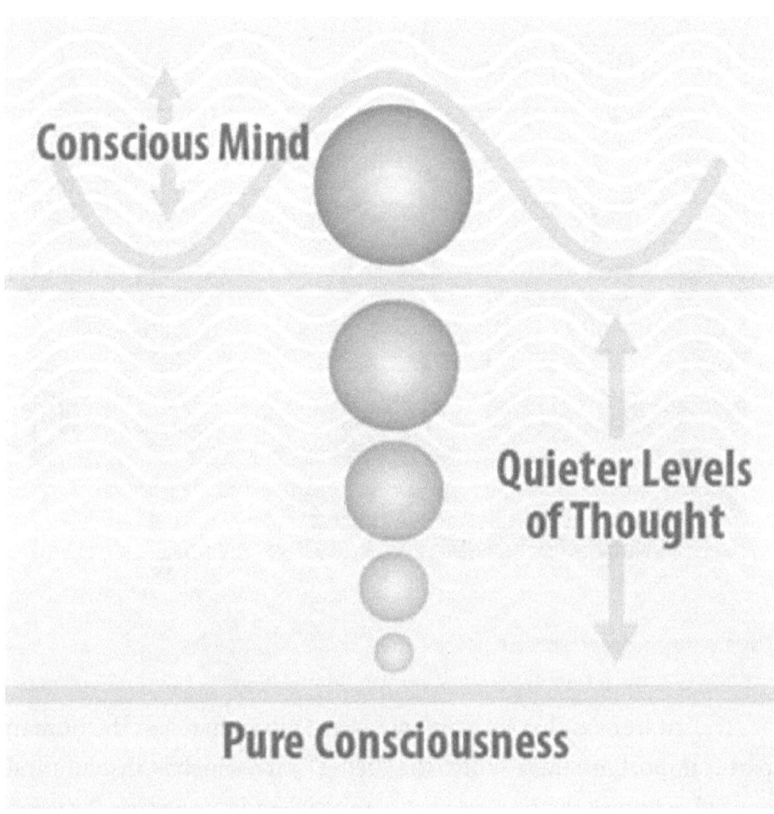

Figure 12: Levels of consciousness of our mind

When we meditate, the pattern of the brainwaves changes. It is known that the "Olympic medal meditators," those with more than 65,000 hours of meditation, are constantly in a heightened state of awareness during which gamma waves are measured. It is also known that when shamans journey within using rhythmic drumming, they access altered states of consciousness. Neuroscience suggests this state may align with the theta brainwave frequency, a state associated with deep relaxation, intuition, and enhanced visualization. Both with meditation and shamanic journeying themes of imbalance, exhaustion, and untapped potential began to surface, inviting us to create harmony from within.

Human Brainwaves

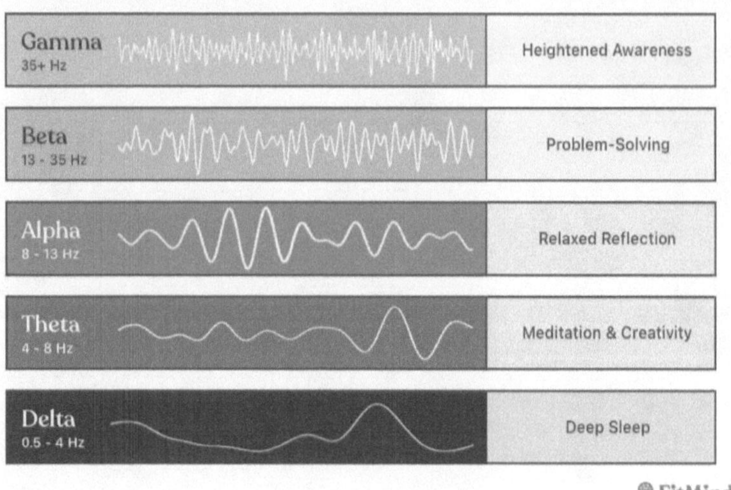

Figure 13: Frequencies of human brainwaves

The awareness that human beings are more than just the human part is important; there is also the "being" part, which is absolute and eternal, whereas the human part is relative and temporary. Between our first breath (birth) and our last breath (death) is what we call our life. Living a life and being aware of our true selves is essential for our spiritual growth. Most of the time there is great suffering before we realize we are more than just flesh and blood.

In my specific case, it took three lower-back surgeries before I surrendered. Before my third and last surgery, I said I would accept the outcome of the surgery, whatever it would be, although it was not a high-risk surgery. By accepting the outcome up front, I surrendered, and I put an end to almost ten years of suffering from lower-back pain, which was actually a gift. Living with a higher level of consciousness is a lifestyle and a choice. It does not come free, and it does not fall from the sky, with the exception of those who are born with a special gift. For most of us, it takes surrendering to a suffering we have carried for many years. The realization is that suffering is not a punishment but a gift—a gift and a choice. It's a choice that we choose to label as suffering. As said in the saying of Buddha in the last chapter: Pain is inevitable, but suffering is a choice. Our mind is of great importance in determining which road we walk in life. We can choose to grow due to pain, or we can choose to suffer.

One of the most remarkable experiments I have seen about how powerful our minds can be in creating a reality occurred during the retreat in Chile for the Energy Medicine Wheel training for the direction of North and East in November 2023. A virtual reality headset was used with a simulation of (1) stepping onto an escalator, (2) the elevator goes to floor 200, (3) at the height of 200 yards, the elevator doors open and there is a springboard of 1.5 yards to walk on. Although you are standing with both feet on the ground, your mind receives signals from your senses that you are standing at an elevation of 200 yards on a plank 1.5 yards long and 0.40 yards wide. You can feel the wind; you have difficulty controlling your balance, because the springboard is 0.40 yards wide. It's amazing what happens to our breath, heartbeat and body temperature. Because our senses are interpreting "danger—200 yards height—falling down," which is actually not reality. Our mind receives the signals, and our breath increases, our heartbeat increases, and our body temperature increases. Some students were heavily shaken, and others tried to jump while both feet were on the ground. When the door opened, my first reaction was danger. My body started to shake, and my heartbeat increased. I kept telling myself, "This is not real. I'm standing with both feet on the ground, and it does not matter how I am stepping forward and backward. There is no risk for me to fall from a 200-yard-high building and die tragically." This proved to be a simple but powerful illustration about how our minds can trick us, creating reality, creating danger, and creating stress that is not necessary. Imagine living your life in the constant reality of danger, threat, and stress. Our body is not built to support such a burden. Our mechanism for fight-or-flight activates temporarily to save us from being killed when the danger is imminent and not when it is perceived. In reality, there is no danger at all. There are many people living in constant threat, with constant enemies, with constant stress, and at the end, they get sick, or they die.

A healthy mind definitely leads to a healthy human being, which leads to healthy nations. The key to living a life fostering a healthy mind is to seek the inner light, the inner peace, the inner calm, the inner abundance, the inner love that is present in all living beings, not only in human beings. The keyword here is **inner**.

So, how do we get to this inner light? We can get there by meditation and by an alternate state of consciousness that shamans use during journeying or plant medicine ceremonies like Ayahuasca. The idea is not that we should visit a shaman constantly, or that we should have a plant ceremony on a regular basis to tap into the inner light. As Villoldo explains in the documentary, "The Luminous Warrior," to dream and experience oneness, our brains must produce melatonin. The production of melatonin in the pineal gland is key and depends heavily on our diet, because melatonin is produced from serotonin, of which 95 percent is produced in our intestine, in our guts. If serotonin production is broken or not functioning properly due to antibiotics or other medicines we take, there is no serotonin production and no conversion of serotonin into melatonin in our brains for the sense of oneness.

Tapping into the inner light is not only meditation and/or shamanic journeying, but it also requires nourishing our body with intelligent food that upgrades our gut and ultimately our brains. In *Grow a New Body Cookbook: Upgrade Your Brain and Heal Your Gut with 90+ Plant-Based Recipes,* Villoldo and Chef Conny Anderson describe 90+ plant-based recipes to activate the intelligence of the inner light.

"You are a new human who can transcend the limitations of genetic inheritance and environment to grow a resilient and vibrant body and brain," say Villoldo and Anderson. The recipes in the book are designed to help you grow younger. They employ the wisdom of the Amazon forest dwellers and will switch on repair-and-regeneration systems that reside inside every cell and organ in your body. The recipes will turn on banks of stem cells ready to help you grow a new body that will defy aging and reduce the risk of disease. The eating plan they offer is based on four principles:

1. Eat a primarily plant-based diet with occasional fish and eggs (no more than once a week).
2. Limit saturated fats (from meat and cheese) and eliminate sugar or anything that turns into sugar in your gut, such as processed grains. Eat a lot of fruits, but only in the afternoon.
3. Eat only two meals a day within an eight-hour eating window. This means skipping breakfast or dinner. Do not eat anything within three hours of bedtime.
4. Supplement with B-complex vitamins, vitamin D, DHA, and a daily multivitamin and mineral formula. Laugh heartily and forgive easily.

Tapping into the light within requires discipline. It is a lifestyle, a daily choice. It is not optional. Once you have been exposed to the light within, it keeps calling you back to be in silence, in peace, in abundance, and in bliss.

"When we pray, we talk to God. When we meditate, we listen to God."
—GABRIEL MEJIA, FOUNDER OF HOGARES CLARET IN
COLOMBIA AND AUTHOR OF *LA TERAPIA DEL AMOR*

With the work that has been done by Foundation Hogares Claret in Medellin and other cities of Colombia, it has been shown that children and youngsters who had a life filled with misery, who committed crimes at a young age, can be saved. Their lives can be changed drastically when their inner light is turned on. Turning on the light within is achieved through true meditation and Yoga at the Foundation Hogares Claret. Medellin, which used to be one of the most dangerous cities in the world during the era of Pablo Escobar in the eighties and nineties, has become an example city for Colombia, winning the most innovative city in the world award in 2013, the Lee Kuan Yew World City Prize in 2016, and the Wellbeing Cities Award in 2019.

BENEFITS OF TRANSCENDENTAL MEDITATION

The scientifically proven benefits of Transcendental Meditation are:

MENTAL HEALTH BENEFITS

- **Stress Reduction.** One of TM's most widely recognized benefits is its ability to reduce stress and anxiety by encouraging relaxation and balancing the nervous system. TM's effects on cortisol levels (the stress hormone) have been studied, with findings often showing significant reductions.[3]
- **Improved Focus and Clarity.** TM is associated with increased focus, memory, and decision-making abilities. Studies show improved cognitive function in practitioners is likely due to the calming effects of regular meditation on the mind.[4]
- **Emotional Resilience.** TM encourages emotional stability and resilience by helping practitioners manage stress more effectively, which can reduce the risk of anxiety and depression.

PHYSICAL HEALTH BENEFITS

- **Heart Health.** Several studies have indicated that TM can lower blood pressure and reduce cardiovascular risk factors. Some health organizations endorse TM as a supplemental practice for managing hypertension and heart disease.[5]

---

3   Aswathy Chandran and N. K. Manjunath, "The Effects of Transcendental Meditation on Cortisol, Anxiety, and Stress," *Indian Journal of Physiology and Pharmacology* 61, no. 4 (2017): 347–52; Antoine Lutz, John D. Dunne, and Richard J. Davidson, "Meditation and the Neuroscience of Consciousness: An Introduction," in *The Cambridge Handbook of Consciousness*, ed. Philip David Zelazo, Morris Moscovitch, and Evan Thompson (Cambridge: Cambridge University Press, 2007), https://doi.org/10.1017/CBO9780511816789.020.

4   David W. Orme-Johnson and Howard M. Chandler, "The Effects of Transcendental Meditation on Creative Thinking," in *Scientific Research on the Transcendental Meditation Program: Collected Papers*, vol. 1, ed. David W. Orme-Johnson and John T. Farrow (Rheinweiler, West Germany: MERU Press, 1977.

5   Robert H. Schneider et al., "Long-Term Effects of Stress Reduction on Mortality in Persons ≥55 Years of Age with Systemic Hypertension," *American Journal of Cardiology* 95, no. 9 (May 1, 2005): 1060–64, https://doi.org/10.1016/j.amjcard.2004.12.058; Deane H. Shapiro Jr., *Meditation: Self-Regulation Strategy and Altered State of Consciousness* (Aldine, 1980); James W. Anderson, Chunxu Liu, and Richard J. Kryscio, "Blood Pressure Response to Transcendental Meditation: A Meta-analysis," *American Journal of Hypertension* 21, no. 3 (2008): 310–16, https://doi.org/10.1038/ajh.2007.65.

- **Improved Sleep.** Many TM practitioners report better sleep quality, fewer sleep disturbances, and relief from insomnia. The calming effects of TM, along with the reduction in stress, contribute to these improvements.[6]
- **Immune System Support.** TM has been shown to have positive effects on the immune system by reducing stress hormones and promoting relaxation, which support overall immunity and recovery.[7]

ENHANCED CREATIVITY AND PROBLEM-SOLVING

- TM allows the mind to rest and refresh, boosting creativity and cognitive flexibility. Studies indicate increased alpha brainwaves, linked to relaxation and creativity, during TM practice, suggesting improved problem-solving abilities.
- Many artists, writers, and professionals report increased creative output and inspiration as a result of regular TM practice, possibly due to the technique's impact on deepening consciousness and mental clarity.[8]

---

6   Fang Wang et al., "The Effect of Meditative Movement on Sleep Quality: A Systematic Review," *Sleep Medicine Reviews* 30 (December 2016): 43–52, https://doi.org/10.1016/j.smrv.2015.12.001; Jayaram Thimmapuram et al., "Heartfulness Meditation Improves Sleep in Chronic Insomnia," *Journal of Community Hospital Internal Medicine Perspectives* 10, no. 1 (2020): 10–15, https://doi.org/10.1080/20009666.2019.1710948.

7   Kenneth R. Eppley, Allan I. Abrams, and Jonathan Shear, "Differential Effects of Relaxation Techniques on Trait Anxiety: A Meta-Analysis," *Journal of Clinical Psychology* 45, no. 6 (November 1989): 957–74, https://doi.org/10.1002/1097-4679(198911)45:6<957::AID-JCLP2270450622>3.0.CO;2-Q; Fred Travis et al., "Effects of Transcendental Meditation Practice on Brain Functioning and Stress Reactivity in College Students," *International Journal of Psychophysiology* 71, no. 2 (February 2009): 170–76, https://doi.org/10.1016/j.ijpsycho.2008.09.007.

8   Sara W. Lazar, Catherine E. Kerr, Rachel H. Wasserman, Jeremy R. Gray, Douglas N. Greve, Michael T. Treadway, Metta McGarvey, Brian T. Quinn, Jeffery A. Dusek, Herbert Benson, Scott L. Rauch, Christopher I. Moore, and Bruce Fischl, "Meditation Experience Is Associated with Increased Cortical Thickness," *NeuroReport* 16, no. 17 (November 28, 2005): 1893–97, https://doi.org/10.1097/01.wnr.0000186598.66243.19; Fred Travis et al., "Effects of Transcendental Meditation Practice on Brain Functioning and Stress Reactivity in College Students," *International Journal of Psychophysiology* 71, no. 2 (February 2009): 170–76, https://doi.org/10.1016/j.ijpsycho.2008.09.007.

SOCIAL AND INTERPERSONAL BENEFITS

- **Enhanced Relationships.** TM has been linked to improved inter-personal relationships, likely because of reduced irritability and enhanced empathy. Practitioners report greater patience, under-standing, and positivity in interactions with others.[9]
- **Sense of Community.** TM communities and groups provide social support and a sense of belonging, which can contribute to personal well-being and a broader sense of a collective purpose.

POTENTIAL SOCIETAL BENEFITS

- **Maharishi Effect.** Although the idea is scientifically debated, the notion that collective meditation can influence societal harmony remains central to TM. Some scientific studies have shown prom-ising correlations, while others remain inconclusive. Nonetheless, this concept has inspired peace initiatives worldwide.[10]
- **Educational and Institutional Applications.** TM is used in schools, prisons, and by corporations to foster a positive, pro-ductive atmosphere. These institutional applications are aimed at improving focus, reducing conflict, and promoting well-being in structured environments.[11]

What happens when life squeezes us? This is a gift to realize where we still need to polish the rough edges of the precious being we are.

Life was squeezing me physically between 2004 and 2015—three lower-back surgeries, and mentally, a great turbulence at ENNIA. Out-

---

9   Michael C. Dillbeck and Kenneth L. Cavanaugh, "Group Practice of the Transcendental Meditation® and TM-Sidhi® Program and Reductions in Infant Mortality and Drug-Related Death: A Quasi-Experimental Analysis," *SAGE Open* 7, no. 1 (January–March 2017): 1–15, https://doi.org/10.1177/2158244017697164.

10 John S. Hagelin et al., "Effects of Group Practice of the Transcendental Meditation Program on Preventing Violent Crime in Washington, D.C.: Results of the National Demonstration Project, June–July 1993," *Social Indicators Research* 47, no. 2 (1999): 153–201, https://doi.org/10.1023/A:1006978911496; David Orme-Johnson and Lee Fergusson, "Research on the Maharishi Effect," An Antidote to Violence, accessed January 15, 2026, https://anantidotetoviolence.org/transcendental-meditation/research-on-the-maharishi-effect/.

11 David Orme-Johnson, "Theory and Research on Conflict Resolution through the Maharishi Effect," *Modern Science and Vedic Science* 5, no. 1–2 (1992): 76–98.

wardly, professionally, everything seemed perfect. I was promoted two times, first from managing director of Amerfoortse Health Insurances to Chief Operations Officer of ENNIA in the first quarter of 2006, and second from Chief Operations Officer to Senior Managing Director. Although my ambition was to become CEO of ENNIA, when the CEO left in 2009, he asked me to succeed him. I said no. My intuition told me ENNIA was not my tribe, not my place to become a CEO, given the risks and noncompliance.

Already in 2011–2012, after the second surgery, I started with a quest about spirituality and my spiritual awakening. Something told me my lower-back pain was not just about getting surgery. By the third surgery in 2015, I had sworn I would never again have a surgery for my lower back—there must be, there should be, another option spiritually. I vowed to find it.

That's when I learned about John of God, the Brazilian healer, in October 2011. John of God, a seemingly average rancher from Aba-diânia, Brazil, offers a powerful message of love, compassion, and hope for humanity. João Teixeira de Faria, the healer and medium known as John of God, allows "spirit doctors" to take over his body three times a week to miraculously treat the thousands of people from all over the world who come seeking a remedy. John of God has fulfilled his mission as a medium for more than forty-eight years, making numerous pilgrimages around the world. Drawn by the hope of instantaneous healing, over eight million believers have stood in front of him throughout his lifetime, as tens of thousands journey to Brazil each year to see John of God and his home, the Casa de Dom Inácio de Loyola (Ignatius of Loyola), which accommodates hundreds of visitors each day.

Ignatius of Loyola is remembered for his deep spirituality, his role in shaping modern Catholicism, and the enduring influence of the Jesuit order, which continues to be active in education, social justice, and religious life today. He was canonized as a saint in 1622. Ignatius of Loyola was one of the many "spirit doctors" that João Teixeira de Faria worked with in the Casa, depending on who was standing before him.

To visit John of God, you must pay for your own travel expenses. The visit to the house of Dom Ignacio is without any cost. João Teixeira de Faria sees patients three times a week, from Monday to Wednesday. On Thursdays and Fridays, he performs special spiritual interventions/ surgeries; most are performed as you walk toward John of God. Once you have arrived in front of him, the spirit doctors have already performed the spiritual surgery.

Everyone visiting the Casa of Dom Ignacio has to be dressed in white. You will be guided toward a current when entering the casa of Dom Ignacio, which is a current of approximately fifty to sixty people sitting in deep meditation. Then you will approach João Teixeira de Faria (John of God), who sits in a chair surrounded by many crystals from the area of Abadiânia, and on the left side and right side, there are always four chairs, eight total, where other mediums sit to hold the energy state as high as possible. Every visitor passes in front of him. The "spirit doctor" who is active in his body as a medium scans the person in front of him physically, emotionally, and spiritually and gives instructions to the guide who accompanies the visitor. The instructions consist of four options:

1. Meditation in the current
2. Crystal bed therapy
3. Natural remedies
4. Spiritual surgery

MEDITATION IN THE CURRENT

This group of visitors always sits in the room before approaching John of God. This is a cleansing area where all visitors are being cleansed, and the energy vibration is raised.

CRYSTAL BED THERAPY

Crystal bed therapy stimulates and boosts the immune system at a high level. It lifts your energy vibration to assist your overall mental, physical, emotional, and spiritual well-being. It cleanses your chakras from any negative energies that have become attached to your energy field. It is known that every disease that appears in the physical body is an imbalance in one or more of the chakras, the energy centers of the body.

NATURAL REMEDIES

Based on the spirit doctor's diagnosis, the visitor receives a prescription for natural remedies sold at the Casa of Dom Ignacio.

SPIRITUAL SURGERY

Based on the spirit doctor's diagnosis, the visitor receives instructions for a spiritual surgery to be performed on a Thursday or Friday. Most spiritual surgeries are done from a distance, while the visitor lies in their room. Only a small group of visitors has to be in the Casa for their spiritual surgery.

In the next chapter, we'll explore the origins of shamanism, the traditions, and the wisdom teachings. I will share stories and practices that have brought these ancient healing techniques alive in my present life.

CHAPTER 14

Shamanism and the Ancient Healing Techniques

My first experience with Shamanism was amazing. It was in Chile in February 2017, and I was there for the "Grow a New Body" retreat offered by The Four Winds Society of Dr. Alberto Villoldo. During a one-on-one session with him, he opened his Wiracocha (seventh chakra) to read my energy body. He then immediately asked me, "Gilbert, tell me about your father." When I told him what had happened that night when I saw my father give my mother a slap in her face, he said, "I know, I can see you have an imprint on your heart chakra. You must release this dense energy, and the Shamans present during this retreat will help you to do that." The next day, I scheduled a session with one of the shamans, and he did an illumination ceremony to release the dense energy in my heart chakra, which had been caused by an action of my father when I was thirteen years old. From that day on, I worked on my relationship with my father until the day he died in February 2023. I stood next to him at the moment of his last breath, and I was at peace that we had restored our relationship and I had forgiven him.

When I booked my first shamanic energy medicine retreat at Four Winds in 2017, I was about to find out how to grow into a new body. It's for those who are feeling the need for a major reset. I wanted to shed unwanted pounds. In 2017, I weighed almost 200 pounds, so this caught my attention. The retreat is for those who want to reach a new level of energy and well-being, and I very much needed that. The promise was that the seven-day retreat would move me to exceptional health "so your health span can equal your lifespan!" Featured modalities at the retreat included detoxifying nutraceuticals to clear away brain fog, boost clarity and energy, and protect your brain.

One key aspect of the Grow a New Body retreat is a vegetarian diet; all carbs are eliminated from your daily intake. This meant no sugars, not even sugar from fruits—except blueberries, which are a powerful antioxidant. It meant no rice and no pasta. On top of eliminating all carbs, early in the morning there was a hiking program in the beautiful mountains of Los Lobos. We were to start hiking at 6:00 a.m. without breakfast. What happens when your body is not taking in sugar and carbs? After two to three days, you enter a metabolic state called ketosis, in which the body uses fat, rather than carbohydrates, as its primary energy source. This process occurs when carbohydrate intake is low, causing the liver to convert fat into molecules called "ketones." These ketones then circulate in the bloodstream and serve as an alternative energy source, especially by the brain, which typically relies on glucose. Normally, the body converts carbohydrates into glucose (sugar), the primary energy source. When carbohydrate intake is significantly reduced, glucose levels drop. Without enough glucose, the body starts breaking down stored fat for energy. The liver converts fatty acids from body fat and food into ketones, which are then released into the bloodstream. Cells, especially in the brain, can use ketones as fuel. In summary, ketosis is a natural metabolic state that can have health benefits, especially for weight management and mental clarity. However, it should be carefully monitored, as prolonged or extreme ketosis can lead to negative side effects, especially in individuals with specific health conditions.

Right away, I could feel the mental clarity and the elevated energy. The morning hikes became a blissful exercise. To be on the mountaintop was to witness a beautiful sunrise. I lost almost 20 pounds in just a week. My belly was gone just like that. I remember I made a bet with my second son, Jorzinho, that I would return home from Chile without a fat belly and with my abdominals looking like six-packs. The fat belly was definitely gone, but to have abdominals like six-packs, I would have to do a lot more abdominal training at the gym. Besides the vegetarian meals and hiking, we had classroom instruction on shamanism in general and shamanism from the Americas specifically.

The objectives of a major reset—shedding unwanted pounds and gaining new levels of energy, mental clarity, and well-being were definitely achieved. I returned home like a new adult—I felt like I was eighteen years old.

After this retreat, my curiosity about spiritual evolution and shamanism soared. I wanted to learn more. I wanted to grow spiritually. I was clearly in the grow-up phase. My desire to grow pushed me to explore more teachings and trainings from the Four Winds Society. I'd return five more times, twice for the Energy Medicine Wheel workshop (February 2020, November 2021); once for a one-day Arsenate trip (June 2021); once for the Amazon One Spirit retreat (April 2022); and an epic journey of Greece (September 2023).

WHAT IS SHAMANISM?

Shamanism is one of the world's oldest spiritual and healing practices, deeply rooted in the animistic beliefs of indigenous cultures worldwide. It is based on the belief that shamans—spiritual guides and healers—can communicate with the spirit world to help individuals, communities, and the environment.

The word Shaman means "the one who knows." Knowing, or "Gnosis" in Greek, is knowledge through experience or insight. It's wisdom, wisdom not from science but from the cosmos or the universe. So the true meaning of "shaman" is the one who knows much more than what we know in the physical world. Their wisdom comes from the plants, the animals, the mountains, the stars, you name it!!!, from God or the universe itself!!

The origins of shamanism date back tens of thousands of years, as evidenced by artifacts and cave paintings that depict figures in trance-like states, animal motifs, and ritualistic scenes. Shamanic practices likely began in Siberia and Central Asia, where the term *Shaman* is derived from the Evenki word *šamán*, meaning "one who knows" or "priest." This concept gradually spread through Eurasia and into the Americas, Africa, and Australasia as human societies migrated and developed independently. Shamanic traditions evolved to suit local environments and cultures, giving rise to a wide variety of practices that share core elements. These elements include the use of trance states, mediation between the physical and spirit worlds, and the understanding that every element of the world—plants, animals, landscapes, even the weather—holds its own spirit and agency.

While shamanic practices vary widely across cultures, they share several fundamental concepts:

1. **Animism and Spirit Belief.** At its core, shamanism is animistic, meaning it posits that all things—living and non-living—are animated by spirits. Shamans work with these spirits to heal, guide, or assist.
2. **Trance and Altered States of Consciousness.** Shamans enter altered states to communicate with the spirit world. Techniques for achieving these states include drumming, chanting, dancing, fasting, or using natural psychoactive substances. The trance is essential for shamans to journey into the spirit world, where they consult with guides, ancestors, or other spiritual beings.
3. **Healing.** Shamans often act as healers, believed to have the power to cure physical, mental, and spiritual ailments. They may perform soul retrievals (recovering lost parts of a person's essence), remove harmful energies, or communicate with spirits to restore harmony.

4. **Rituals and Ceremonies.** Many shamanic practices involve elaborate ceremonies that often take place at sacred sites like mountains, rivers, or forests. Rituals often include chanting, dancing, drumming, and offerings to spirits. These practices are believed to honor the spirits, maintain harmony, and aid in the transition between life and death.

5. **Connection with Nature.** In many traditions, shamans act as stewards of the environment, respecting the interdependence between humans and nature. They may serve as mediators between their communities and nature spirits, ensuring balance and sustainability.

6. **Use of Sacred Objects and Symbols.** Shamans frequently use objects, such as drums, rattles, feathers, and stones that are believed to carry spiritual power. Symbols and animal totems also play a central role, often representing the spirits or forces a shaman works with.

SHAMANISM AND HOLISTIC MEDICINE TODAY

Worldwide Shamanism is present in different cultures. Today, shamanism has undergone a revival as interest in indigenous wisdom, nature-based spirituality, and alternative healing has grown globally. It is practiced widely beyond its original cultural contexts, and "neo-shamanism" or "modern shamanism" has emerged as a movement blending traditional practices with contemporary life.

NEO-SHAMANISM AND THE NEW AGE MOVEMENT

- Neo-shamanism, prevalent in Western cultures, adapts traditional shamanic techniques for personal healing and spiritual exploration.
- It emphasizes individual transformation, often through workshops, retreats, or online courses.
- Modern practitioners may use drumming, guided meditations, and animal spirit guides as methods for personal insight.

- Unlike traditional shamanism, neo-shamanism often lacks the rigorous cultural context and apprenticeship system, focusing more on psychological and self-help aspects.

AYAHUASCA AND PLANT MEDICINE TOURISM

Ayahuasca is a brew made from plants, and its effects come mainly from two key chemical components working together: DMT (N,N-Dimethyltryptamine) and Beta-carbolines (MAO inhibitors). Both are needed in Ayahuasca because the Beta-carbolines inhibit monoamine oxidase (MAO) in the gut and liver. This prevents DMT from being broken down. In our guts we produce 90 percent of serotonin, which is transported via the gut—brain axis to our brains, and serotonin is converted into melatonin when we sleep. Melatonin is converted into DMT, which is an active component of Ayahuasca, which gives us the visionary/psychedelic effect and allows us to sense the Oneness (Unity) with every being on the planet.

- The use of ayahuasca has become popular globally, with people traveling to the Amazon or attending retreats worldwide to experience the visionary effects of the plant medicine.
- These experiences are often guided by trained shamans or facilitators, and they aim to address deep-seated trauma, addiction, and personal growth.
- This form of tourism is controversial, as the commodification of indigenous practices can lead to ethical and cultural concerns.
- However, many traditional shamans work to protect their knowledge and create ethical frameworks for sharing plant medicine with outsiders.

INTEGRATIVE AND HOLISTIC MEDICINE

- Some medical and psychological practitioners integrate shamanic techniques with conventional treatments.

- Practices such as breathwork, mindfulness, and even nature therapy draw on shamanic concepts of connecting with oneself and nature.
- Certain therapists are trained in shamanic journeying techniques, which they use to help patients explore subconscious issues or access deeper parts of themselves in a therapeutic context.

ENVIRONMENTAL AND SOCIAL ACTIVISM

- Shamanic teachings are influencing environmental and social activism, as many contemporary practitioners advocate for the stewardship of the earth based on shamanic principles of interconnectedness.
- Shamans are often consulted by indigenous activists, particularly in regions such as the Amazon, where they collaborate to protect their homelands and bring attention to the global environmental crisis.

MODERN CHALLENGES AND ETHICAL CONSIDERATIONS

- The resurgence of shamanism in non-indigenous contexts raises ethical questions, including cultural appropriation, the commercialization of sacred practices, and the authenticity of neo-shamanic practitioners.
- Traditional shamans often undergo extensive training and inherit their roles through rigorous processes that modern practitioners may lack.
- Furthermore, the global interest in shamanism has led to debates about protecting indigenous intellectual property, as some communities seek to safeguard their traditions from exploitation.

Shamanism is a profoundly influential spiritual and healing practice with roots extending back thousands of years. Though often adapted to fit contemporary needs, its core principles remain focused on the interconnectedness of all life and the human responsibility to care for the earth and its inhabitants. As shamanism continues to evolve, it bridges ancient wisdom and modern consciousness, offering valuable insights for those seeking personal transformation and a deeper connection to nature.

THE FOUR WINDS SOCIETY

Years ago, the medical anthropologist Dr. Alberto Villoldo spent years in the Amazon rain forest, hoping to find the bark or root that could become the next great cancer cure. After all, the jungle is nature's pharmacy, filled with exotic plants whose powers have yet to be discovered. Villoldo spent many months canoeing to villages that had seldom seen a white man. Wherever he went, he found there was no cancer, dementia, or heart disease, even among the elders of the communities. Clearly, the indigenous people of the area knew something about health that we Westerners didn't know. What was their secret?

Shamans believe everything we perceive is a mirror of an internal map or blueprint that we call reality. These maps are stored in what scientists call neural networks in the brain, and what shamans define as the Light Body or Luminous Energy Field (LEF). The LEF can be thought of as the software that informs your DNA—the hardware—to repair your body. Ordinarily, your LEF shapes your health (and your emotional scripts) according to the instructions inherited from your parents—it replicates the heart conditions, the breast conditions, and the emotional dramas that cut across generations. By working directly with the energetic matrix that informs the human body, and all living things, we can break free of this inheritance and create a new destiny.

"The luminous energy field contains a blueprint of how you will heal, how you will age, and how you might die. Energy medicine creates the conditions for health, so disease goes away, or never happens." Clear the imprints of disease from the Luminous Energy Field, extract intrusive energies and emotions, and heal traumas.

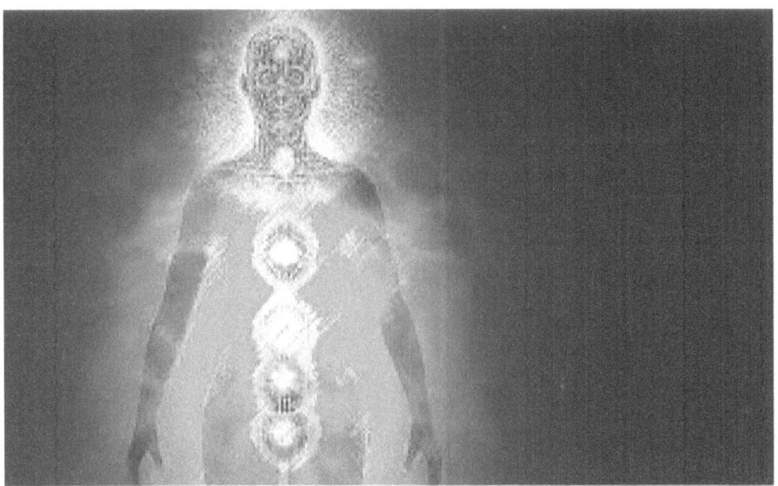

Figure 14: The chakras and the luminous energy field

The LEF consists of seven chakras:

FIRST CHAKRA

- Location: At the base of the column and connected to the column
- Color: Red color
- Element: Earth
- Keyword: I am (Female, mother)
- Function: Security
- Age of Development: Between zero to seven years
- First Chakra is our root

SECOND CHAKRA

- Location: beneath the belly bottom
- Color: White
- Element: Water
- Keyword: I feel (Male, father)
- Function: control of power and center of power
- Age of Development: Between seven and fourteen years

THIRD CHAKRA

- Location: Above the solar plexus
- Color: Yellow
- Element: Fire
- Keyword: I do (Our will)
- Function: Who am I? The search for individuality
- Age of Development: Between fourteen and twenty-one years

FOURTH CHAKRA

- Location: Heart
- Color: Green
- Element: Air
- Keyword: I love (affirmation) and I can see you
- Function: Intimacy
- Age of Development: Between twenty-one and twenty-eight years

FIFTH CHAKRA

- Location: Throat
- Color: Blue
- Element: Ether
- Keyword: I search for the truth
- Function: Finding your purpose, communicating your purpose and passion, and connecting with subconsciousness
- Age of Development: Between twenty-eight to thirty-five years

SIXTH CHAKRA

- Location: Forehead
- Color: Indigo
- Element: Light
- Keyword: I perceive
- Function: Intuition (Third Eye)

- Age of Development: Between thirty-five and forty-two years

SEVENTH CHAKRA

- Location: Above the head
- Color: Violet
- Element: Subtle Light
- Keyword: I am creator and curator
- Function: Development of spiritual maturity
- Age of Development: Between forty-two and forty-nine years

EIGHTH CHAKRA

- Location: Sacred space
- Function: Sacred bridge (Quecha name = *Wirachocha*)

The LEF has four layers extending outward from the body. These four layers are:

1. Causal (the Spirit)
2. Psychic (also known as etheric—the soul)
3. Mental-emotional (the mind)
4. Physical (the body)

Each layer stores a different quality of energy. The outermost layer stores the energy that fuels the physical body. The layer beneath stores the energies that sustain our mental and emotional stamina. Underneath this layer are the refined psychic energies, and closest to the skin is the finest energy of all, our spiritual fuel reserves. The mystical literature refers to these layers as "subtle bodies." In reality, they are not separate from each other, in the same way that the colors of the rainbow are not disconnected but rather dissolve into one another.

The LEF contains an archive of all our personal and ancestral memories, of all early-life trauma, and even of painful wounds from former lifetimes. These records, or imprints, are stored in full color and intensity of emotion. Imprints are like dormant computer programs that, when activated, compel us toward behaviors, relationships, accidents, and illnesses that parody the initial wounding. Our personal history indeed repeats itself. Imprints of physical trauma are stored in the outermost layer of the LEF. Emotional imprints are stored in the second layer, soul imprints in the third, and spiritual imprints in the fourth, and deepest layer. Imprints in the LEF predispose us to follow certain pathways in life. They orchestrate the incidents, experiences, and people we attract to ourselves. Imprints propel us to re-create painful dramas and heartbreaking encounters yet ultimately guide us toward situations wherein we can heal our ancient soul wounds. All imprints contain information, which informs the chakras, which then organize our physical and emotional world. The information in an imprint organizes the luminous energy field, which later organizes matter. The LEF contains a template of how we live, how we age, how we heal, and how we might die. When there is no imprint for disease in the LEF, recovery from an illness happens at tremendous speed. By the same token, imprints for diseases can depress the immune system, and it can take an extremely long time for us to regain our health during an illness. None of us wants to spend months convalescing when we could have recovered in a matter of days or weeks. When we erase the negative imprint that triggered the onset of illness, the immune system can rapidly eradicate the disease.

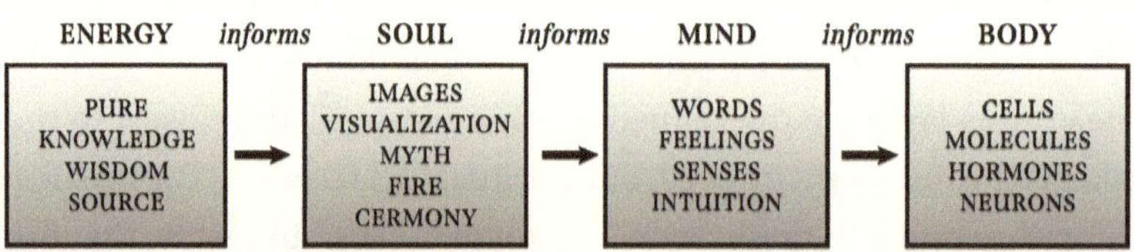

Figure 15: The four levels of energetic engagement

Shamans intervene at the energy level, because at this level transformation takes place instantly. It's where the magic occurs, and diseases will disappear before appearing in the physical body. The other way around is what we have been doing in the Western world; we try to cure a disease in the physical body. At Four Winds Society, the wisdom energy healing was condensed in the Energy Medicine Wheel training.

ENERGY MEDICINE WHEEL

When I read the information about the energy medicine wheel program on the website of Four Winds Society, I knew instinctively this was a program that I must enroll in: "spirit was calling me."

The description on the website of Four Winds of the program was:

Do you want to discover how to clear the imprints of disease from the Luminous Energy Field, extract intrusive energies and emotions, and heal trauma in yourself and others?

Do you want to know how to up-regulate the energy matrix that informs your body, switch off the cellular death-clock responsible for premature aging, and the genes that create disease?

Do you want to know how to detox the body and brain, and upgrade the LEF in order to grow a new body that ages gracefully, heals rapidly from trauma, and dies consciously?

Do you want to help yourself, clients, and loved ones attain and maintain exceptional health, help others die gracefully, and help families recover from loss?

In 2020, these questions were all answered with a solid yes. I was immensely drawn to this wisdom—it felt like it had been a part of me all the time, but I had lost the connection. The qualities of a peacemaker I described in Chapter 2, and that little voice that was always present in me was saying, Yes, yes, let's do this.

So I booked my second retreat at Four Winds in February 2020. Normally the Energy Medicine Wheel training is for four consecutive weeks, but due to my busy schedule as CEO of a new hospital that just became operational less than three months ago, it was not possible for me to be away for four consecutive weeks. I'm glad I didn't, because after my two-week retreat, I experienced how the first COVID-19 patient had died in the intensive care department of Curaçao Medical Center.

The teachings of the energy medicine wheel program are summarized as follows: at the end of the Energy Medicine Wheel program, each student will have learned, according to the center:

- The science of energy fields
- How to turn wounds into sources of wisdom and compassion
- How to reset the fight-or-flight system to feel safe in the world
- The shamanic fire ceremony
- The rites of passage and initiations
- The Illumination Process
- Shamanic tracking skills
- Soul Retrieval
- The Extraction Process
- The Great Death Rites
- Dying Consciously

Being a student of the Energy Medicine Wheel program in February 2020 for the South and West directions and in November 2021 for the North and East directions expanded my spiritual knowledge and boosted my spiritual growth enormously. As indicated in Figure 15, shamans recognize four levels of engagement and four levels of universal powers. Each of these four levels is identified by archetypes that manifest at specific levels of engagement in the universe, in physics (gravity, electromagnetism, and nuclear force), and in biology (the four-letter code of DNA). These are the same four powers that manifest in both the physical and biological worlds. Once this relationship between the four powers is understood, then shamanism is understood.

THE ILLUMINATION PROCESS

Direction: South

The practice of shamanic energy medicine: our body

Archetype: Snake

Shamanic energy medicine upgrades the quality of the Luminous Energy Field and instructs our cells and our genes to express health. The Illumination Process is the core practice of energy medicine. It is systemic healing of your physical body and your emotions. I learned to clear toxic energies from the chakras and to overwrite the imprints that predispose us to disease. LEF is actually the light body that we bring with us from lifetime to lifetime. I learned how to clear the karma and history of violence and suffering encoded in the LEF.

Through the Illumination Process, we can switch off the genes that create pathology and erase the imprints of disease from the LEF. Our body will grow a new body that heals and ages gracefully and can help our loved ones and eventually clients to heal from toxic emotions and prevent disease. Our bodies in the physical world are being regulated by cells, molecules, organs, hormones, and neurons.

The archetype used for the south direction is the snake. Why the snake? Because the snake teaches us how to shed our skin. Unlike humans, who continually shed skin cells, snakes shed their skin in one large piece and do so periodically. This is called ecdysis. The main reason snakes shed their skin is to allow further growth and to remove parasites. A snake's skin doesn't grow with its body.

This is used as a metaphor for the south to teach us that, as we grow in life, we have to let go of old habits, thoughts, and traumas that are obstacles to our further growth.

Practices of the South are:

- **Nonjudgment.** Nonjudgment of yourself or others. Practice discernment. Break free of conceptual reality. Step into experience not preconceptions.
- **Non-attachment.** Not holding onto old perceived ways things are or need to be. Practice beginner's mind. Be free to experience the world. Don't take yourself so seriously.
- **Non-suffering.** Life has pain—suffering is what we do before and after the fact. Live life in the moment not anticipating outcomes.
- **Walk in beauty.** Practice beauty as expansiveness. Touch everyone you meet with beauty. Come back to the garden.

These are essential practices to have a life as light as possible, not with too much weight and luggage due to judgment, attachment, and suffering. One of the powerful sayings of Buddha is: "Holding on to anger is like drinking poison and expecting the other to die." We don't have to hold on to anger. We have to let go and practice nonjudgment, non-attachment, and non-suffering.

In each direction, traditional rites are passed to each student. For the South direction, the following rites are given:

- Kawaks—seer rites
- Ayni karpay—archetype seeds in each chakra
- Hampe rites—rites to mesa; a mesa is the altar of a Shaman
- Bands of protection—energy bands to protect your luminous energy field from intrusive energies

THE EXTRACTION PROCESS

Direction: West

The practice of shamanic energy medicine: our mind

Archetype: Jaguar

Shamanic energy medicine allows you to leave behind the tired, worn-out stories and illnesses of your family of origin. The shaman learns to shed the death that has been selected for him by culture and genetics. Extraction of the old stories and illnesses is fundamental to breaking out of the bell curve and not becoming a statistic that has to die with Alzheimer's, cancer, or cardiovascular disease. The Extraction Process clears the biological and karmic imprints of your family of origin as well as the emotional legacy inherited from your ancestors and former lifetimes. It clears the intrusive energies of earthbound spirits trapped between this world and the next, which can attach themselves to a person, and express their ailments through them. Through Shamanic Journeying, you learn to visit three former lifetimes. You learn to clear the karma brought into this lifetime so you can die peacefully and consciously. In the training of the West, you also learn the journey beyond death.

Our mind is based on our five senses and is regulated by words, feelings, and thoughts. The unhealthy mind is described in previous chapters as creating psychosomatic disease, but our healthy mind can create psychosomatic health.

Why the jaguar as an archetype? Because the jaguar is fearless. One of the main enemies of humans is fear, and living with fear constantly. Fear shuts down everything in our natural human lives, and ultimately, we get sick. The jaguar lives without fear in the jungle and is a master of its environment, knowing everything about its habitat and where and when to hunt fearlessly.

PRACTICES OF THE WEST

- Fearlessness
  - To actively practice peace and nonviolence
  - Not responding from a place of anger or fear
  - Not colluding with the consensual reality (maintaining a high level of integrity)
  - Not unconsciously agreeing with what everyone else is doing
  - Motivated by a powerful state of ethics
  - Not ruled by everyone else's beliefs
- Non-Doing

- Immerse yourself in the flow of the universe
    - Stay in the present
    - Rather than pushing to make things happen, allow things to unfold
  - Practice of Certainty
    - Have an unwavering commitment to the course you've chosen
    - Leave no backdoors open—burn your bridges
    - Don't create what keeps you from being fully engaged in your present
    - "If this doesn't work, I can always…"
    - No doubt, absolute trust in spirit, fully stepping into your life with no escape hatches
  - Practice of NonEngagement
    - No longer engages in predatory relationships
    - Violence no longer lives within us
    - Select your battles carefully. Ask: Is this conflict worth my energy?

For the West direction, the following rites are given:

- Pampa Mesayok Rites—Caretaker of the Earth—Day keepers

Like the jaguar takes care of his natural habitat, the Pampa Mesayok rite teaches us to take care of the earth, to be day keepers of the earth.

In February 2020, two months after the COVID-19 pandemic started in China, it was one month before the first patient died in Curaçao Medical Center (CMC). For that reason, the energy medicine wheel training felt predestined for me to participate. After the Grow a New Body retreat in February 2017, a lot happened that changed my life for the better.

I quit my job at ENNIA four months after that retreat, intending to take a sabbatical. However, when spirit calls, we have to respond, and spirit called me twice: first for the refinery, and later for the new hospital. The retreat of the Energy Medicine Wheel in February 2020 for the South and West directions prepared me to shed old habits and thoughts to become fearless ENNIA after fourteen years of employment without having any job offers. However, I was sure it would be fine. I completely trusted the journey that great spirit had defined for me.

THE WAY OF THE ANCIENT WISDOM

Direction: North

The practice of shamanic energy medicine: soul retrieval

Archetype: Hummingbird

Shamanic energy medicine teaches us how to master time and step into infinity so we can fix things before they manifest in the world. The mystery teachings become available to us once we begin our healing journey. The North direction teaches us the practices of Invisibility, Mastery of Time, and Keeping a Secret.

In the North direction, we learn how trauma can cause soul loss, where a part of our essential self lives, and the wounded self remains behind. When this happens, our destiny is derailed, and we fall into the grip of fate. The problem with fate is that it is pre-ordained. We are no longer free, and we become victims of our genetics, our karma, or the tragic stories from our childhood. This is where transgenerational traumas are amplified. We will be living the stories of our parents and their parents and their parents. This is basically what has been happening with the children of parents who came from transatlantic slavery. We still live our lives today with the stories told and taught to our great-great-grandparents of envy, which has its root cause in the "rule and divide" policy introduced during wars in Africa, which was maintained by slave owners. This trauma manifests itself in the so-called "crab in a barrel syndrome." We are not our stories. We must become the storyteller. Mastery of Time teaches us how to step into infinity to fix things before they are born. Just as a person can track a deer through the forest, you learn to track into the past to discover an ancient wound that needs to be healed today. Or to track into the future to find a healed state that can reach back like a giant hand and guide the person to the health and well-being they seek.

The hummingbird holds rich symbolism and spiritual significance across cultures and spiritual traditions. Its unique characteristics—its ability to hover in place, fly backward, and move at astonishing speeds—make it a compelling symbol of resilience, joy, and connection to the spiritual world. Hummingbirds are known for their strong connection to calling from spirit. When great spirit calls, they respond. Some species respond by travelling thousands of miles during migration, representing endurance and adaptability. They consume up to twice their body weight daily to fuel their energy-intensive flight. Their ability to hover symbolizes being present in the moment.

PRACTICES OF THE NORTH

The Practice of the Beginner's Mind:

- Simplify—reduce the clutter at every level.
- Serpent—literally clear out the excess stuff.
- Do not be possessed by your possessions.
- Jaguar—clear limiting beliefs.
- Hypothetical relationship of the world.
- Hummingbird—stop identifying with your thoughts.
- Take every belief about the nature of reality and throw it in the fire. Then we are free to reinvent ourselves and our world.
- Eagle—find spirit.
- Engage your life as a love: "Thank you for life and for each moment."

Practice of Living Consequently:

- Every word, thought, and action sends out vibrations.
- Each of these has consequences.
- Hold the full awareness of your actions and the ripples in time.

Practice of Transparency:

- Allow oneself to be completely seen with nothing left to hide.
- Stop hiding the parts of yourself that make you uncomfortable.
- Be transparent, completely congruent—walk your talk.
- Do not explain yourself—it's OK if they don't get who you are.
- Don't be a target—there's no need to be right.
- Become conscious of your beliefs.
- Choose being useful and valuable.

Practice of Integrity:

- Be true to your word and recognize its power to create reality.

For the North direction, the following rites are given:

- Alto Mesayok Rites—Wisdom Keepers Rites, Mountain Rites.

The Alto Mesayok are the ones who communicate with the mountains and are the wisdom keepers of the world.

THE WAY OF THE VISIONARY

Direction: East

The practice of shamanic energy medicine: the journey beyond death

Archetype: Eagle

Through shamanic energy medicine, we can dream our world into being. For the shaman, the world is always mirroring back to the condition of her love and her intent. When your love and intent become pure, the world reflects this back to you perfectly. This is what we call reality. In the North direction, we learn that everything we perceive is simply a reflection of the condition of our love. So to change the world, we change the map of reality within. Full of energy, we want to change the world full of wisdom—we want to change ourselves. The journey beyond death is central to shamanic teachings worldwide. The North direction teaches us practical tools to help a loved one who is passing return to the world of spirit consciously, without any unsaid "I love you" or "I forgive you." We learn to set the luminous body free and bring consciousness with us at the moment of death—a practical skill we will all need one day.

Having gained knowledge and techniques in the North and East directions in November 2021, they became valuable to me in February and August 2023 when both my father and mother passed away. The teachings of shamanism gained during the "Grow a New Body" retreat in February 2017 helped me practice forgiveness with my father after I was unable to speak to him for almost three decades. It was truly a beautiful experience to make his last meal for him the day before his death and to be with him at the moment of his last breath. I was able to guide him through death, where our luminous body is set free from our physical body. Although I experienced pain—pain for not having my father present anymore in physical form, I was happy that I was present during his last breath and could thank him for everything he had done for us, and tell him how much I love him.

The death of my mother was slightly different because she chose to leave this world. She had no medical condition that would lead to her death, but she chose to stop eating and lived like that for months. With her strong character, she demanded the food she loved. Sometimes it took hours to prepare the meal, and she just took one spoonful. Then she would say, "I'm full," or "It's not tasty enough," or "It's too tasty." Our love and patience for her was tested during these months. It was beautiful to see after all those months, she requested our permission to go. We had to set her free and thank her for everything she had done for us, and tell her how much we loved her.

One day after we gave her permission to leave, she passed away. I was the only one present when she took her least breath. She could no longer speak because of the severe pain after months of not eating, but she left in peace.

The year 2023 was truly a death and rebirth year for me—the deaths of both my parents within six months, but I experienced my rebirth with their strength, wisdom, and love to become a storyteller of the indigenous wisdom.

Because we dream the world in constantly—let's dream an incredible world.

PRACTICES OF THE EAST

Mastering Time:

- Step into the stream of timelessness. Let go of the restrictions of the cause-and-effect paradigm.
- Recognize you live in a sacred time. The universe conspires on your behalf.
- Practice Ayni—being in a proper relationship to life.
- Step outside of time into infinity and perfection, being informed by that.
- Practice stillness so you can create movement and shift your momentum tunnel.
- Practice Owning Your Projections: Awareness.
- Practice awareness that you are creating your world in every moment.
- Recognize what you have created, and what you now choose to create.
- Recognize the mirror the universe is reflecting on your behalf.
- Discover and acknowledge the parts of yourself that you've refused to look at.

Practice of No-Mind:

- Break free of your thoughts and get in touch with the sage within, who is beyond thought.

Practice of Indigenous Alchemy:

- Move through the four-step transformational process around the Medicine Wheel.
- Move to the point of no longer addressing issues that are only in our lives.

THE AYAHUASA CEREMONY

During the training of the East direction in November 2021, Marcela Lobos arranged an ayahuasca ceremony for me. Ayahuasca is a brew that has been used for centuries by the indigenous people of the Amazon for vision quests. The major psychoactive ingredient in ayahuasca is N,N-Dimethyltryptamine (DMT), a derivative of serotonin, which is produced naturally in our body, in the pineal gland. The main purpose of our brains is to help us dream and create a higher level of consciousness. DMT helps us sense and experience oneness—the sense that we are all connected to every being, because every matter is energy, and we are light and energy beings.

The master of the ceremony was a traditional shaman from the Shipibo tribe of Peru. The program was three sessions of ayahuasca, and every session was one night. The first night was on a Friday, and it was a full moon. I went up to the hill in the building where physical exercises are done. There was one tour guide and the Shipibo Shaman, who was the master of ceremonies that night. He explained the ceremony to me in detail: how it begins, the chanting of the Icaros, and which songs are sung to amplify the effect. These Icaros songs originate from the spirit of the three of which the ayahuasca brew is made.

The shaman lit candles, started smoking a traditional cigar, and then poured a small portion of the ayahuasca brew into a small glass. He asked me to have the most clear and purest intentions, and then I could drink the brew. After that, you should wait a while to experience the effect. I waited for thirty to forty-five minutes, and then I felt like I was going to vomit. I tried to contain it, but I didn't succeed. After approximately one hour of drinking the ayahuasca, I vomited like never before. I almost felt like my whole stomach and intestines were coming out. During my two weeks at the North and East direction, the meals were vegetarian and very light, and yet my body was already on a vegetarian diet. But still I had to vomit.

After the ceremony, the Shaman told me I had some cleansing to do, to let go of all the old emotions and energies that I still kept in me. After a while, I stopped vomiting because there was simply nothing more to vomit. The ceremony ended after approximately three to four hours. During all that time, the shaman sang the Icaros. After the end of the ceremony, we said goodbye, and I went to my room. I could sense some lightness in my head and my body. My stomach felt completely drained after the vomiting.

The next ayahuasca ceremony was the next Sunday, and the same procedure was followed. The shaman gave me the same portion of ayahuasca to drink, and like the night before, the waiting time starts from this moment. But this time it was different. After thirty minutes my senses were amplified. I could feel how the Ayahuasca brew was moving from my stomach into my intestines. The sensation of vomiting was not present at all, and I felt my intestines absorbing the ayahuasca brew. Not long after the absorption, I felt like my body was dissolving. I put my right hand in front of my face to be sure of the sensation, and I saw all my fingers and the hand dissolve like sand in the ocean, like sugar in a glass of water. Piece by piece my body was being dissolved, and I started to sense an immense light, so immense that it could not be ignored. I was part of this light, and there was no separation because the only thing left of Gilbert was light, my luminous energy field, my soul.

My soul and I were surrounded by light and love, unconditional love. I was surrounded by the universe—I was the universe. I could see and hear the Icaros songs clearly. I could see many planets of the universe and other lifeforms—we are definitely not alone in this universe. Starting with the mentor of Villoldo, Don Manual, I could see the whole lineage of the medicine men and women of the Q'eros from

Peru going back thousands of years. All their faces flashed like a movie at high speed. I could feel and sense everything they had experienced since the arrival of Europeans in the Americas. All that time I was asking myself what was happening to me, and then I realized I was having an out-of-body experience. I was completely stripped of myself/ Gilbert. The only thing that was left was my soul to experience **the oneness with the universe and all beings**, that we are all connected and that there is no separation on the fourth level of engagement, the energy level. There is only a separation of our bodies and our minds.

The light and love I have experienced out of my body have truly poured me with love, unconditional love. It has increased my consciousness level in a way that is difficult to explain with words. You can watch movies on GAIA and read books about people having an out-of-body experience or a near-death experience, but it doesn't come close. Experiencing this without dying and suffering is a blessing. A blessing and a gift that should not be kept to myself but should be shared with the world. We can definitely create a better world—we must do our utmost to create a better world—a world free of anger, hate, fear, and jealousy, a world based on love, unconditional love. Not love based on a return or a favor but unconditional love. During my out-of-body experience I have seen and felt how love is present everywhere in the universe, at the same intensity and frequency, without discrimination.

The training of the Energy Medicine Wheel was truly a life-changing event for me—both on a personal level (death of my parents) and on a professional level (CEO functioning at the hospital of Curaçao). Working in a public function with great hostility and media attacks, this ancient wisdom helped me remain calm and transition from student to master. It helped me become a storyteller of this powerful and beautiful ancient wisdom, which can be used as indigenous alchemy to transform the lives of all humans on this earth who are ready to make this transition.

TWO-DAY AUSANGATE TRIP

In June 2021, Marcela Lobos became my mentor. I was ready to continue my wake-up, seeking more knowledge and more experience. I had two more trainings ahead—the last two directions (North and East) in November 2021. But before that, she had arranged a two-day trip to Ausangate, a place of profound spiritual significance for the Q'ero people, the last surviving Incan descendants who reside in the high Andes of Peru. This majestic mountain, standing at over 20,945 feet, is not only the tallest peak in the Andes, but it's considered a living deity and one of the most sacred Apus (mountain spirits) in Andean spirituality. Apus are sacred mountain spirits believed to possess immense power, wisdom, and the ability to influence human lives. Ausangate is revered as one of the most powerful Apus (supreme Apu), embodying the protector of the region and a provider of life through its glaciers and streams. For the Q'eros, mountains like Ausangate are not just physical features but gateways to the Pachakuti, or the Andean concept of cosmic order. It connects the earthly plane (Kay Pacha) to the spiritual realms above (Hanan Pacha) and below (Uku Pacha). Ausangate is thought to align with celestial forces, serving as a conduit for energy between the cosmos and the Earth. This connection highlights its role as a mediator between humans and the divine.

I flew from Curaçao to Lima, Peru, and then from Lima, Peru, to Cusco. It is a 53-mile drive, and the sights are beautiful. We passed through villages where the traditional Cuy is eaten, an animal similar to a Cavia. After arrival at the base camp, the shamans held a fire ceremony during which a *despacho* (offering) was burned for Ausangate. It was extremely cold—I had a sleeping bag but still could not sleep at night; it was too cold. The toilet was outside the house, so imagine you have to pee at night, and your body just starts to warm up, and you have to go outside where it is below zero degrees Fahrenheit. It was freezing, and I was praying the night would pass by as soon as possible.

Marcela arranged for Pascual Apaza Flores to be my lead shaman. Pascual is an Alto Mesayok, and he speaks directly to the mountains. When I arrived in Cusco, the altitude was already affecting my breathing. I walked from my hotel to Plaza de Armas, where the statue of Pachacutti stands, and I was exhausted. It was not even a thirty-minute walk. It took me a couple of hours to acclimatize. Ausangate was even higher than Cusco—Cusco was 3,399 yards above sea level, and Ausangate was 6,300 yards above sea level, which was almost double. Therefore, that evening at the base camp of Ausangate, the regional shaman suggested I have a horse as a backup during the walk to Ausangate because being exposed at such low temperatures, at such a height, and at such low levels of oxygen could become an issue for many people. It was a six- to seven-hour walk, visiting three different lakes and doing ceremonies, mainly one fire ceremony where a *despacho* was being burned during the fire ceremony. It was an *agni despacho*, with agni meaning to be in the right relationship with every living organism around us.

Figure 16: Retreat at Ausangate mountain in Peru

The main message and lesson I received from Ausangate was that I have to speak only when necessary. This message came to me after the fire ceremony of the *agni despacho*.

After the two-week retreat for the North and East directions in November 2021, Marcela invited me to participate in the Amazon One Spirit retreat in April 2022 at the EcoAmazonia Lodge, which is nestled within the 500-acre Tambopata ecological reserve in the Peruvian Amazon rainforest. To reach the lodge, we took a two-hour boat ride along the Amazon River (Madre de Dios) basin, departing from Puerto Maldonado, known as Peru's capital of biodiversity. The fifty bungalows at the lodge were designed and built with local materials following standards of environmental and social responsibility. The retreat's main activities included early yoga or chi-kung; hiking along the rainforest with a resident botanist; healing baths and cleansing with the shamans; and evening ayahuasca ceremonies.

The Amazonian rainforest was magical. It had always been on my bucket list to spend time there. I was most impressed by the botanist, who told me in detail which tree, flower, leaf, and root of a plant is used for all kinds of diseases and treatments. The healing baths and cleansing with shamanic sessions offered deep healing. They featured the leaves of the plant *Ruda* and an extract of the flower *Cananga*, both from the region. The leaves of the Ruda are removed from the branches and broken into small pieces. The broken leaves are then put in a large barrel with water. The extract of the Cananga is mixed with the broken leaves of the Ruda. This mixture is used as a bath. Every student can pour the mixture over their body after using the leaves of the Ruda as a natural soap to clean the whole body.

I enjoyed being in the presence of the three Shipibo shamans, two females and one male, from the Pucallpa area, from which the Shipibos come. In the evening, ayahuasca ceremonies were organized for those open and ready to experience an ayahuasca ceremony. The retreat offered four ayahuasca ceremonies, and I participated in three. In none of those three ceremonies did I have an experience comparable to my experience during the ayahuasca ceremony in Chile. For me, it was a sign that the medicine plant showed me what unconditional love really feels like, and I explored the universe in its true essence and the ancient lineage of the Q'ero tribe.

THE EPIC JOURNEY OF GREECE

Next, I went to Greece in September 2023. Here is how Marcela described the retreat in the flyer:

> When the outer landscape has the power to favorably impact our inner world, it is worth considering it a place of pilgrimage. The Four Winds Society has handpicked destinations to facilitate deep transformation for groups and individuals. The epic journey to Greece is to Eleusis, Delphi, and Delos, where some of the most interesting and transformative mysteries of ancient Greece were revived. Storytelling ceremonies, sacred medicine, nature walks, and meditation are the ingredients of the daily practices. In Eleusis, the inevitable descent to the underworld is contemplated for renewal. In Delphi, the sacred place of the Oracle, deep questions of the soul can be asked. In Delos, the wisdom of the past is woven into the tapestry of the enlightened future. We follow the footsteps of the ancient seekers who searched for the meaning of life, inquired into the journey beyond death, and sought revelations from Gods in caves, oracles, and temples of Gnosis. Imagine all of this draped over the portal of Equinox, amplifying the epic proportions of this adventure.

I felt tempted, but first I had to tell her I wanted to think about it because I was grieving my father, who had died in February 2023. Our oldest daughter, Aimee, finished high school and was preparing for her trip to the Netherlands to study medicine. On top of that, my mother had two surgeries and was not eating properly, retaining a lot of fluid in her legs, with the consequence that she could no longer walk. I was in doubt, but despite all the doubts and turbulence, I knew intuitively I had to go on this epic journey to Greece. Something was calling me to be there during the fall equinox of 2023, and I'm glad I went. Like all the other retreats, it was a life-changing event. The idea of writing this book was strengthened during this retreat. During two nights we had SOMA ceremonies, and during the second night, I had a blissful experience being surrounded by healers receiving their wisdom, light, and unconditional love.

WHAT IS SOMA?

Soma is a term rich with meaning in the Indian tradition. Soma is praised as a god in the Rig Veda, as the full moon, and as a substance, which the gods ingested to gain immortality (synonymous with the term *amrita*), as written here. "We have drunk Soma and become immortal; we have attained the light, the Gods discovered…Absorbed into the heart, be sweet, O Indu, as a kind father to his son, O Soma, As a wise friend to friend: do thou, wide-ruler, O Soma, lengthen out our days for living. These glorious drops that give me freedom have I drunk…Make me shine bright like fire. Give us a clearer sight and make us better." Some regard the hymns of the Vedas about Soma as purely metaphorical, while others believe they refer to an actual substance consumed by the priests during the rituals. Several plants have been proposed but it is still a debated issue, as every candidate is disputed for some reason. Whatever the word might have referred to, Soma suggests something of a high nature, something that opens the way toward spiritual dimensions of reality while also enhancing the quality and capacity of our lived experience. It is, in a certain sense, the very essence of life and the blissful quality of an awakened consciousness. "By dwelling, abiding and living in the eternality of the Absolute, taste, know, experience and receive the bliss of the nectarian Soma" is a translation of a Vedic verse by Paul Muller-Ortega.

This epic journey to Greece yielded two pivotal insights.

Well, I could not have received messages (insights) from the spirit world that were more applicable to my personal life. The appearance of Atlas carrying the whole world hit home. I had been working for fourteen years at an insurance company, feeling like I was the one responsible for safeguarding its moral compass. My involvement at the refinery was also about a moral compass, where bribery was the central topic of the forensic investigation. Finally, yet importantly, my involvement in the transition from the old to the new hospital and later as CEO of the new hospital was also a battle over my moral compass and injustice. Injustice from the local government of Curaçao to assume their responsibility and allocate an adequate healthcare budget for the new hospital instead of playing the blame-and-shame game.

Indeed, during all those years, my inner voice told me these executive positions were not my end station. They were temporary, and I was being prepared for something else—something where I can serve humanity with what I do best: live in peace and harmony with myself and with our environment, to live in "Agni," as the shaman says. The need for spirituality in business and the world is immense. It is immense for keeping the focus on what really matters rather than just the material part. My journey to seek my light within has brought me the teachings of transcendental meditations from Maharishi Mahesh Yogi and the ancient knowledge of shamanism from the Americas from Villoldo. For me, it is time to share my knowledge and experience with anyone who is open to receiving this ancient knowledge for true healing. I'm grateful I listened and followed my intuition when spirit was calling me. I'm grateful I decided to attend the retreat in Greece, where the seed for my book was germinated.

THE EPIC TRANSFORMATION JOURNEY OF PERU 2025

In July 2025, I traveled to Contamana, Peru, for a healing ceremony for my prostate. A shipipo shaman named "Mama Ida," who has been in Peru for the Amazon One Spirit retreat, has a son, Angel, close to the lake Tipischka. I took a flight from Lima, Peru, to Pucallpa, and from Pucallpa, it was a boat trip on the river Ucayali of 6.5 hours, a lovely journey with beautiful views. As explained in the Introduction "Death and Rebirth," my dad died of prostate cancer in February 2023.

My dad told me that almost all of his uncles died of prostate cancer. So I knew there was a lineage of unresolved wounds, traumas, and patterns passed down through my dad's line, and ancestral healing was key to releasing this energetic lineage. Ancestral healing is a spiritual, psychological, and sometimes ritual practice focused on addressing unresolved wounds, traumas, and patterns passed down through family lineages. The core idea is that our ancestors' experiences—such as grief, violence, colonization, displacement, or even unexpressed love—can leave imprints that ripple through generations, shaping behaviors, health, and emotional patterns in their descendants.

Mama Ida and Angel agreed to prepare a special retreat program for me, focused on healing my prostate. The program consisted of a special liquid intake of herbs, saunas of special herbs, and three Ayaguasga ceremonies. I arrived at the retreat on a Saturday and started with my dedicated retreat program on Sunday with the intake of an extract of herbs, "to clean your prostate," as Angel told me.

On Monday evening, I had my first Ayahuasca ceremony in Maloka on the property of Angel. I took only half a glass of the brew because the first session was for diagnostic purposes, Angel told me. After thirty minutes, I sensed my consciousness was expanding, and I saw the luminous energy field of every living being, including the trees. Every sound of every night animal was ten times more profound to my ears, and the stars in the sky were shining. Angel and Mama Ida kept singing their Icaros the whole night. Then after approximately two hours, the ceremony was over. I went back to my room, and my consciousness and energy field were extremely open and connected to every being. It was beautiful because every sound of the jungle was magnified. At a certain moment, I felt that I had to throw up. The next day, Angel asked me how I slept. She explained that they had to clear my stomach of a dense energy that was present, and the next ceremony on Wednesday evening would open my vision completely. On Wednesday evening, at the beginning of the ceremony, I took a full glass of the Ayahuasca brew and lay down after a while, patiently listening to the beautiful Icaros songs that Angel and Mama Ida sang.

I did not feel an expansion of my consciousness, and I was not feeling well either. I could not lie down. I could not sit. I was uncomfortable. After 1.5 hours, I decided to step up and walk to the restrooms outside the Maloka to see if I could throw up, which didn't happen. After ten minutes, I went back inside the Maloka and lay down on my right side, my favorite sleeping position. Then it was like a snapshot that my consciousness expanded. I started to see anacondas (snakes) all around me—little ones and the biggest ones. I could feel their energy. I could smell them, and I could even see where they were sleeping in the lake. It was an amazing experience to see how energetically I became one spirit with the anacondas in the lake. At the same time, I started to throw up; it felt like everything in my body was coming out. This energetic integration lasted for at least forty-five minutes, and I felt how symbolically I was leaving my old skin and receiving a new skin. This process is called "ecdysis" or "shedding" or "molting." At the end of the ceremony, which lasted at least three hours, Angel came to me and asked how I was feeling. I told him about my energetic integration with the anacondas, and then he told me they opened my vision completely, which was blocked.

When I returned home, I waited approximately two months for my next PSA blood test. The PSA value refers to the level of Prostate-Specific Antigen (PSA) in the blood. My PSA value has been increasing since March 2022, when I first started to monitor my PSA value due to the development of my dad's prostate cancer. PSA is a protein produced mainly by cells in the prostate gland; a small amount naturally circulates in the bloodstream. The PSA test is a blood test that measures how much PSA is present, and the results are reported in nanograms per milliliter (ng/mL).

The PSA value indicates:

- Low PSA (generally under 4 ng/mL): Usually considered normal, though age and prostate size can affect this.
- Borderline or mildly elevated PSA (about 4–10 ng/mL): May indicate benign conditions such as:

- Enlarged prostate (BPH)
- Prostatitis (inflammation/infection)
- Or early prostate cancer

- High PSA (above 10 ng/mL): Increases the likelihood of prostate cancer, but is still not definitive.

The result on August 25, 2025, two months after the retreat, showed a clear decrease in PSA from 11.2 (June 2025, before the retreat) to 10.38 (August 2025: after the retreat). For me, this was a clear confirmation that the treatment at the retreat was successful. In the West, whenever the PSA value is higher than ten, doctors inform the patient they have a 50 percent chance of having prostate cancer, and the patient has to do a biopsy. During the biopsy procedure, a piece of tissue from the prostate is taken to analyze whether it is benign or malignant. I knew from my energy training at Four Winds that energy organizes matter, and that due to the lineage of my father's ancestral healing, it was necessary to release inherited trauma. In essence, ancestral healing is about making peace with the past to free the present and future. So I had to make peace and forgive my father's bloodline completely. For me, the decrease in three years of steady increase of my PSA value was an indication of how my healthy mind and my energy field, which were cleared from imprints (old skin of the snake), created psychosomatic health for my prostate and released the history of prostate cancer of my dad's lineage from my energy field. It was a challenge to resist the advice of the West to have a biopsy vs. the ancient wisdom that healing occurs on an energetic level. I'm glad I chose wisdom instead of information and data. I was the living example of the ancient wisdom I have learned. I made peace with my past (my father's lineage), to free my present life from prostate cancer and to free my future life from suffering and eventually dying from prostate cancer. That's the essence of ancestral healing, a powerful wisdom from the Shamans, which is not based on data.

So, let's remember that the shaman, according to Villoldo:

Is a person of knowledge and power.

Uses power and knowledge in service.

Knows that love is the organizing principle of the universe.

Knows that creation is not complete—we help dream the world into being.

Is one who has not left the Garden, is not separate from nature.

Knows everything is infused with spirit, with life.

Sees the organizing principle of the universe, the archetypes.

Is in service for the good of all beings and the Earth.

Has a high sense of ethics—works through intent.

Knows and faces the shadow, both personal and collective.

Holds and creates sacred space.

Even with intent, does not fix the outcome—no attachment to result.

Knows that power can heal and also destroy, and uses power wisely.

Knows to work at source—at the energetic level.

Knows we are here not only to grow corn but to grow gods.

Knows that everything is light bound into matter.

Knows that being present with intent can shift the world.

Lives in synchronicity.

Lives with impeccability.

Knows that if you don't learn it, you marry it (get wedded to it), or it comes to you as fate.

Knows that thought directs energy—energy directs matter.

Knows that will is control and that intent is surrender.

Understands the universe to be benign—not predatory. The universe conspires on your behalf.

Knows that "Reality is those myths we can't quite see through yet."

Looks for confirmation in nature and synchronistic events (signs, omens).

Knows that when you call spirit, spirit answers, and when spirit calls, you must answer.

How can we tap into the light within both individually and collectively? How can we transform our wounds into assets and become storytellers of our story instead of telling the story of our parents, our ancestors, community, and culture? That's coming up in the final chapter.

CHAPTER 15

One Light Within Can Light the World

In ancient Greece, women were forbidden to study medicine until one day someone broke the law. Born in 300 BCE, Agnodice cut her hair and entered Alexandria's medical school dressed as a man. While walking the streets of Athens after completing her medical education, she heard the cries of a woman in labor. However, the woman did not want Agnodice to touch her, although she was in severe pain, because she thought Agnodice was a man. Agnodice proved that she was a woman by surreptitiously removing her clothing and helped the woman deliver her baby.

The story soon spread among the women, and those who were sick began to go to Agnodice. The male doctors grew envious and accused Agnodice, whom they thought was male, of seducing female patients. At her trial, Agnodice stood before the court and proved that she was a woman, but this time, she was sentenced to death for studying and practicing medicine as a woman.

Women revolted at the sentence, especially the wives of the judges who had given the death penalty. Some said that if Agnodice was killed, they would go to their deaths with her. Unable to withstand the pressures of their wives and other women, the judges lifted Agnodice's sentence, and from then on, women were allowed to practice medicine, provided they only looked after women.

Thus, Agnodice made her mark in history as the first Greek female doctor, physician, and gynecologist. This plaque depicting Agnodice at work was excavated at Ostia, Italy.

Figure 17: Agnodice at work delivering a baby

This story tells us the importance of speaking up and being united. It's an illustration of one healthy mind that changed history. One brave light within (Agnodice) decided to help another human being in need, risking her own life. Her actions subsequently caused immense jealousy, and she was brought to trial. At her trial, once again her bravery "to do the right thing," showing she was a woman, almost caused her death, had it not been for the wives of the judges who stood up collectively.

"Wrong is wrong even if everyone is doing it, and right is right even if no one is doing it" is a quote often attributed to American civil rights leader, William Penn. To do the right thing even if our own life is at risk takes great courage, but more importantly, it takes a human being with a strong light within, a strong purpose, and someone willing to die for their actions if necessary.

Throughout history there have been many stories like the one of Agnodice, where someone stood up and spoke against injustice to protect human rights. Our local hero on Curaçao, Tula, did that on August 19, 1975, when he said, "We have been abused too much, we do not seek to harm anyone, and we are just seeking our freedom. French Negroes gained their freedom, Holland was occupied by the French, then we must be free here."

They did not seek to harm anyone—they were just seeking their freedom. The revolt of May 30, 1969, was also about injustice, equal pay for equal work, respect, and recognition. In May 1977, when twelve children from the neighborhood Groot Kwartier and surrounding areas were initially not admitted to the school, my mother, Rubia Juliana, and other parents rebelled. They did not rebel with a revolt and destruction but with enough force and attention to the local governmental authorities that they succeeded in ending this absurd discriminatory rule. The rule that was applied until that year mandated that children from the neighborhood of Groot Kwartier and surrounding areas would not be allowed to attend the school because the achievements of the school would deteriorate.

One day back in 2005 after my migration to Curaçao, my mother gave me two old pages from 1977 with the names of twelve children and told me the story of what happened back in 1977. On the left side of the last page, my mother wrote in Papiamentu: "Muchanan ku no a keda aseptá"—which means "The children that were not admitted." To me, this shows one light within or many lights within that changed our future. I am grateful for the parents who stood up for their children.

During my fourteen years of employment at ENNIA, after the switch of new shareholders, I was involved in many internal battles and challenges to prove that the policy of the shareholders was not beneficial for the clients of ENNIA. It was not an easy task because the peer pressure to "act normal' as if nothing was happening was huge. "Everything is okay and don't be ridiculous, you are paid a good salary," I was told. It was true that I was paid a decent salary for tasks and responsibilities that were expected according to my job performance. It was not true that I was being paid a decent salary to accept irregularities and injustices.

This is a huge challenge nowadays because our world has become a place where power and money are the main external forces shaping all levels of our societies. Power and money are externally driven factors with no limitations. There is no limitation to power, and there is no limitation to the amount of money we desire to have. As soon as our moral compass, our internal light, is not on, we will be guided and driven by external factors like power and money. This will destroy us, and it can destroy societies and communities, as shown in previous chapters.

My appointment as president of the supervisory director of RdK, the local refinery, was also about irregularities—the irregularity of bribery and corruption with a death warrant as one of the attempts to stop the work. My involvement at the new hospital, initially as managing director for the transition and later as CEO, was also about menace and manipulation—the crab barrel syndrome.

All these stories and experiences have one thing in common: Being able to stand up, speak up, and preach general interest instead of personal interest when power, money, and deception create a culture of fear. We know what fear does with our minds and our bodies—it rips everything that is good of our mind apart. It is not easy to stand up and speak under such circumstances. The only way we can stand up and speak is when our light within is on and burning, when we are living a life based on our true purpose instead of a life based on our ego. Change starts with *you* and it starts from within. To change, we must first change our mind. As long as we keep thinking the same and doing the same things, change will not happen.

A higher force than the limiting worldly desires that are tempting us constantly is guiding us. It is there, it was there, and it will always be there because that's who we are—we are light beings experiencing a human life for our personal spiritual journey. We have to be brave; we have to seek our light within because that is our beacon, which is our strength and our moral compass.

Our lives and decisions will be so easy and fluent when we are guided by our true self instead of our false self. One of the metaphors I like to use for workshops and motivational speeches is that sunrise is always in the east and sunset is always in the west. Our location is irrelevant—it does not matter if we are in the USA, South America, China, Greenland. or Australia. The directions for sunrise and sunset are always the same. This gives us orientation when we are disoriented, and it gives us guidance; it is universal. There will be no sunrise in the south or sunset in the north ever.

The same is true with our moral compass, our internal light: It is universal. The conditions or locations where we are at that moment in our lives is irrelevant. It's amazing to see how many people change their decision depending on what is at stake. If you ask, for example, if the stake is $1, $1 million, or $1 billion, it would influence the out-come of their decision, most people would say yes. This means in the metaphor of the sun that depending on your location in the world, depending on what's at stake ($1, $1 million, or $1 billion), the choices we make are subjected to what's at stake. That ignores our internal light or moral compass. This ignorance in time will cost us our health, our happiness, and our lives. It took me three lower-back surgeries before I surrendered to whatever the outcome would be of my third lower-back surgery. I was living a life in an environment that was not part of my tribe.

Once you search for the inner light, the true self, and you find this inner light, the true self, there is no going back. This is the phase that Villoldo calls the "**wake up phase**" in the documentary "The Luminous Warrior." We wake up from a dream, from a life that we are living in which we thought "This is it!" and we realize there is more to life. We grasp that we are missing key components in our life, questions such as why we exist and what our purpose is. After the wake phase comes the **"grow-up phase."** We have to grow spiritually, and to grow spiritually, we need to have a lifestyle in which we not only feed our body and mind with healthy food, healthy habits, and healthy relationships, but we also feed our soul with the necessary ceremonies and retreats to keep growing spiritually. The last phase is the **"show-up phase"** where our moral compass is being tested in circumstances of fear or even threats to our lives as was the case for Agnodice, and as I have also experienced at the refinery with the death warrant. We will be exposed to situations in which we have to choose between "right or wrong." These are the most challenging moments in life from my own experience, because this moment will define who we truly are and will separate us from "the herd."

A STORY OF HOPE

Healthy Minds, Healthy Nation is a story of hope that we can and must create a better world for our future generations and for all living beings on this beautiful planet. We must cherish the life we have been allowed to live, the years between our first breath and our last breath. Our behavior as human beings has caused so much suffering and damage to our planet. We can and must learn from all this to make a choice to create a better world every day. Every human being who is guided by the light within, the true self, can help another human being tap into the light within.

A healthy mind is a state of mental well-being where a person can:

- Think clearly and rationally, making sound decisions.
- Regulate emotions effectively, experiencing a full range of feelings without being overwhelmed by them.
- Cope with stress and bounce back from adversity (resilience).
- Maintain positive relationships and engage socially in meaningful ways.

- Stay focused and present with a balanced perspective on life.
- Have a sense of purpose, direction, and self-awareness.

It's not about being happy all the time, but about being able to experience life with clarity, flexibility, and emotional balance. A healthy mind is a quiet sanctuary within, where peace, clarity, and compassion dwell. It is a space where thoughts arise without judgment, and emotions are honored without attachment. A healthy mind is in harmony with the soul, aligned with truth, and open to the present moment. It sees life not as something to control, but as something to flow with. It cultivates gratitude, forgiveness, and inner stillness. It listens deeply—to the self, to others (all beings), and to the divine whisper that guides us from within. In a healthy mind, love is the compass, and awareness is the light.

In his latest book, *Grow a New Brain*, published December 10, 2024, Dr. Alberto Villoldo blends neuroscience, nutrition, and spirituality, offering a comprehensive plan to rejuvenate brain function, enhance mental clarity, and even regrow neural pathways. The book reflects a unique collaboration between Dr. Perlmutter, a neurologist and functional medicine expert who writes the foreword, and Dr. Villoldo, a medical anthropologist and shamanic healer. Together, they merge Western scientific insights with ancient spiritual practices to propose a holistic blueprint for cognitive regeneration.

I will now briefly describe some of the most important themes and concepts of the book. They are fundamental to the idea of standing up and speaking for what you believe in. Once you have a healthy mind and have changed your thoughts, then your spoken words will change as well. From there, your actions will change. You will recognize injustice and have the courage to stand up. If you are living a life of fear, based on scarcity, you will never stand up because you will be too afraid of the consequences of your actions.

So, now let's look at how Dr. Villodo shows us the way to "grow a new brain."

NEUROGENESIS IS POSSIBLE

One of the book's core messages is that brain cells can regenerate, contrary to long-held beliefs.

Through the right combination of diet, lifestyle, supplements, and spiritual practice (prayer, meditation, and shamanism), the brain can grow new neurons and neural networks, even in adulthood.

THE MODERN BRAIN IS UNDER SIEGE

Chronic stress, sugar-rich diets, inflammation, poor sleep, and sedentary lifestyles are degrading our brain function.

The authors describe how the modern environment is causing an epidemic of "brain fog," memory loss, anxiety, and depression.

In the Amazon, the rate of dementia is one out of one hundred people (1 percent), in America it is one out of five people (20 percent). This is a significant difference that has a huge impact on the healthcare costs, not only in America, but worldwide.

THE BRAIN-BODY-SPIRIT CONNECTION

Dr. Villoldo emphasizes the energetic and spiritual health of the brain, drawing on shamanic traditions. Practices like meditation, breathwork, fasting, and vision quests are presented as tools to cleanse the brain and awaken consciousness.

THE FOUR PILLARS OF BRAIN REGENERATION

The four pillars of brain regeneration are a holistic approach that allows the brain to not only resist decline but also actively regenerate and "upgrade itself."

DETOXIFICATION

- Clear the brain of harmful toxins like heavy metals, pesticides, and inflammatory compounds.
- Emphasizes detox tools such as:
  - Glutathione and alpha-lipoic acid
  - Infrared sauna use
  - Intermittent fasting
  - Detoxifying herbs and supplements

NUTRITION AND SUPPLEMENTATION

A ketogenic-style, low-glycemic, high-fat diet is encouraged to fuel the brain.

Key nutrients and supplements include:

- Omega-3 fatty acids (especially DHA)
- Probiotics and prebiotics
- B vitamins, magnesium, zinc
- Curcumin, resveratrol, and other anti-inflammatory agents

NEUROPLASTIC TRAINING

Incorporate exercises and habits that stimulate the brain and improve mental function, such as:

- Learning new skills (languages, instruments)
- Memory games and puzzles
- Physical exercise, especially aerobic and strength training
- Breathwork and meditation to calm the nervous system

SPIRITUAL AWAKENING

This aspect differentiates the book from other neuroscience guides.

Shamanic techniques reset the energetic field of the brain and body.

Practices like soul retrieval, energy medicine, and sacred rituals help readers become "luminous beings."

I have been living my life based on these four pillars of brain regeneration since February 2017, when I participated in the retreat "Grow a New Body" in Chile. I can testify this lifestyle is life changing; I can feel the vitality, the energy, the clarity. I think it would have been impossible for me to deal with all the pressure and stressful environments I have experienced in the past. "When spirit calls, we have to answer," I often say. Spirit will take care of everything you need for the duties ahead of you after answering that call. and guess what? You will become a better version of you, a version of your true self instead a version of your egocentric self.

A STORY OF FAITH

Pain is inevitable in life. We will all experience pain in life, physical pain or pain due to the loss of a beloved person. Suffering, however, is a choice. It's a choice every day that we make to suffer due to a related pain. I was in this mode for many years due to my lower-back pain, questioning why this was happening to me, asking why does everyone have a healthy back except me? Why can't I sit for hours in meetings without experiencing lower back pain? But along my awakening journey, I have learned that it's not about the question Why is this happening *to me*?, but Why is this happening *for me*? I had lost my father and my mother in the same year, within a period of six months. Losing the presence of both your father and mother within six months could have been a source of great pain and suffering. But I chose not to suffer and to have full confidence that the death of my parents was for a specific reason. I trusted they had left me/us in their physical form, but they were present in their spiritual form.

Shortly after my mother's funeral, she confirmed this to me when I asked my parents during a vision quest in Greece, "Where are you?" She answered, *"Mi yu, nos ta tur kaminda,"* which means, "My son, we are everywhere."

We must have faith that pain is a gift—a gift for our growth. Pain is not a punishment. There is something that we can and must learn in this lifetime, and this lesson comes with pain. As my mother used to say, "*Kada pa kiko tin su pasombra.*" Everything happens for a reason. If humanity starts turning on our internal light, if humanity starts helping each other to turn on our internal lights, we can and will create a better world for our future generations and all living beings on this beautiful planet. We need to have the faith that we can and will create a transformation, as the prophecy of Pachacutti tells us in *The Luminous Warrior.*

A STORY OF LOVE

Healthy Minds, Healthy Nation is a story of love—a story of unconditional love given to us as children by our parents, in their own way, with their strengths and weaknesses. The love that formed and educated me was abruptly destroyed that night when I saw my father slap my mother's face. Now I tell a story of love. It took me decades before I could face my father again and forgive him for that trauma. Now I tell a story of love for my life that guided me to find my true love, my queen Chantal. Now I tell a story of love about our five children and how privileged we are if we find this unconditional love in life. We share and grow together through all the ups and downs of a marriage with a combined family of five children. What holds everything together is love, even in times of great turbulence, being surrounded by a family who loves you for who you are. This fuels your journey with energy. Love is the universal language that heals everything. Being exposed to unconditional love changes your life forever. That was the case when I was stripped of my ego during my first ayahuasca ceremony, and the only thing left was my soul to experience unconditional love. If we succeed in globalizing unconditional love, we will literally have heaven on earth.

A STORY OF HEALING: CURAÇAO

What are the chances in a lifetime of mankind that descendants of human beings from West Africa will live on a small island in the Caribbean because of the trauma of the transatlantic slave trade? What are the chances in the lifetime of mankind that a group of indigenous people of northern South America called Arawak migrated from northern South America to a small island in the Caribbean that was called *Las Islas Inútiles*—"The Useless Islands" by the Spanish because it lacked the gold they were seeking? The exact origin of the name "Curaçao" is debated, but several theories exist.

- **Portuguese Influence.** One popular theory suggests the name comes from the Portuguese word *cura*, meaning "cure." Early sailors may have named it after the island's fresh fruits or herbs that helped cure scurvy during long voyages.
- **Indigenous Origins.** Another theory posits that Curaçao derives from an Indigenous word, possibly related to the Caquetío name for the island.

Figure 18: Indigenous map of the islands of the Caribbean

Curacaute was the indigenous name for Curaçao, and it includes the word *cura*. It is not a coincidence that these two primary influences have shaped the history of Curaçao. I believe Curaçao has a hidden secret that was discovered a long time ago, but we have forgotten. Curaçao as an island holds great healing energies that have been ignored for too long. From a collective point of view, there is a lot of healing work to be done for the inhabitants of the island of Curaçao, and actually throughout the whole Caribbean for the descendants of the transatlantic slave trade. Yet as I have said before, pain is inevitable, suffering is a choice, and healing from pain has become a trauma; in our case transgenerational traumas are a blessing. It's a beautiful transformation from rage and hate to compassion and wisdom. It is our lesson during our earthly walk to grow spiritually and realize we are not here to accumulate wealth, but we are here to spread love.

"Darkness cannot drive out darkness, only light can do. Hate cannot drive out hate, only love can do." That was one of the most powerful sayings of Martin Luther King Jr.

Pain is inevitable, suffering is a choice, and healing helps to discover our true purpose and strengthens our inner light during our earthly life. May we, together, find healing for all our traumas in life.

Figure 19: Martha Abbot and me after a Shamanic initiation and Fire Ceremony at the Sanctuary Los Lobos Chile

Conclusion

I had such a Western view of the world when I left Curaçao to study in the Netherlands. Traumatized unconsciously by the divorce of my parents, I wanted to be successful. I wanted to have a big house, a big car, and enough money to do whatever I wanted. I came back to Curaçao, worked at a company where I was earning more than enough money, and was confronted with pain and suffering that led me to have three lower-back surgeries. The lower-back pain was so intense between the first and second surgery that I was desperate. All the joy of earning enough money was gone, because I could not spend it. Then I met my queen Chantal during a turbulent period for the insurance company ENNIA, where the slogan "Feel Secure" was a challenge due to solvency deficits. For an insurance company, being insolvent is devastating because being insolvent means not being able to pay the obligations of clients in the future. This was my beginning, a search for quitting the mind and a more meaningful perspective on a life of wealth that led me to meditation and shamanism.

Is it a coincidence that my queen Chantal and I met at ENNIA? Is it a coincidence that from her ancestry DNA test, 56 percent of her ancestors are from Benin and Togo, and for me, 66 percent? I don't think so. Our ancestors have been together long before we could ever imagine being together. Is it a coincidence that a small island in the Caribbean, discovered by Indigenous Arawaks from South America, conquered by Spain, England, and the Netherlands, has been a major port for the transatlantic slave trading, where the slaves from West Africa arrived on the island in great pain, suffering, and trauma? Is it a coincidence that I was involved in three major integrity challenges (ENNIA, Refinery, and new hospital) during the last decade on the island of Curaçao? Is it a coincidence that one of the names of the island of Curaçao is the island of healing?

I'm convinced these are no coincidences but perfectly arranged events in time from great spirits, from the universe, both for me on an individual level, and for the island Curaçao on a collective level, the region, and the world. I think the wisdom of the indigenous Shamanistic approach is already out there in the West because humanity realizes we cannot keep living as we have been doing during the past centuries. We have to become a better version of what we are; we have to experience a Pachacutti. Life could not only be the worldly, perishable, and materialistic things we desire based on power and money, and based on our ego. There must be more in the lifetime of humanity that we are just starting to see and realize that the way of thinking and the systems we have created are not sustainable.

Quiet the mind and discover the light within. Quiet the mind and discover our true self, our soul, instead of our ego. Quiet the mind and create a healthy mind. It's not only a matter of quieting the mind, because if we quiet the mind but we keep feeding our body with unhealthy food, fast food, for example, we will still have an unhealthy mind. We will become what we eat. Our body is our temple of light and energy. We have to take care of our body and our soul, because mind, body, and soul are deeply interconnected.

If we change our thoughts, we will change our lives. If we change our lives, we will change the world. In the West, we have been educated and driven by individuality and success; wealth is measured by parameters that have nothing to do with wealth from a spiritual point of view. We have been driven by individuality and disconnection from nature instead of the force and union of community and connection with nature. Dr. Alberto Villoldo tells the story of a shaman living in a cage overlooking a beautiful valley and river who was visited by a group from the west.

One of the westerners asked the shaman, "How could you live in such a cave, in poverty and such miserable conditions?"

The shaman invited the westerner to the entrance of his cave, which overlooked a beautiful valley and answered, "How can I live in poverty and have a miserable life? Look at this valley; look at the mountains; look at the rivers. I'm the wealthiest person on this planet."

When the Dalai Lama was asked what surprised him the most about humanity, he answered, "Man sacrifices his health in order to make money, then he sacrifices money to recuperate his health. And then he is so anxious about the future that he does not enjoy the present; the result being that he does not live in the present or the future; he lives as if he is never going to die and then he dies having never really lived."

I hope that *Healthy Minds, Healthy Nation* will serve as a source of inspiration, a source of hope, a source of love, and a source of healing. I hope that humanity will heal all our suffering and traumas, so we can become a better version of ourselves, a better version for our family, our community, our country, and for the world. I hope this better version of humanity will create a better version of the world based on love and abundance instead of power, money, and scarcity. Pain is inevitable, suffering is a choice, and healing helps us discover our true purpose and strengthens our inner light during our earthly life. May we, together, find healing for all our traumas in life.

Further Reading

Part I: A Foundation for a Healthy Mind

Chapter 3, Ego vs. True Self

Ego is the Enemy, Ryan Holiday (Penguin Press, 2016).

The Undiscovered Self: The Dilemma of the Individual in Modern Society, Carl Gustav Jung, (Routledge & Kegan Paul, 1957).

Chapter 6, What Does It Mean to Be a Peacemaker?

Emotional Intelligence—Why It Can Matter More Than IQ, Daniel Goleman (Bantam Books, 1995).

Part II: How Unhealthy Minds Create Unhealthy Nations

Chapter 9, The Impact of Traumatic Events on the Mind, Brain, and Body

The Body Keeps the Score: Brain, Mind and Body in the Healing of Traumas, Bessel van der Kolk (Penguin Books, 2014).

Part IV: Ancestral Healing Wisdom

Chapter 13, Transcendental Meditation

Science of Being and Art of Living—Transcendental Meditation, Maharishi Mahesh Yogi, (Plume, 1963).

Chapter 14, Shamanism and Ancient Healing Techniques

Grow a New Brain, David Perlmutter and Alberto Villoldo (Hay House, 2023).

Grow a New Body: How Spirit and Power Plant Nutrition Can Transform Your Health, Alberto Villoldo (Hay House, 2016).

Chapter 15, One Light Within Can Light the World

Acknowledgments

I gratefully acknowledge the unconditional love of my mother, Rubia Juliana, who raised me with discipline, moral integrity, and the way to fight for justice, who even after her passing said to me in a vision quest, "*Mi yu, nos ta tur kaminda*—My son, we are everywhere."

My father, Gilbert Martina, for his passion for cuisine and music, and his strong connection with Mother Nature. May their souls rest in peace.

I would like to thank Marcela Lobos and Alberto Villoldo for bringing the wisdom of the ancient Q'ero Incas from America to the world, my teachings during the retreats with Four Winds Society, and especially to Marcela Lobos for being my coach and mentor during the creation of *Healthy Minds, Healthy Nation.*

Carolyn Flynn, author of *Boundless* and developmental editor with The Story Catalyst, who as my editor has been the best ally and support I could have as a starting author, crafting my thoughts from a book proposal and subsequently to a book—what a warm-hearted professional that challenges you to be the best you can be. Kelly Notaras, Founder of KN Literary Arts, and Amy Hosford, General Manager of KN Literary Arts, for assigning me to the best editor I could have hoped for on the project. Katie Lathrop, my publishing manager from Scribe Media, for her marvelous project management skills. Katie Mcintosh and Rachel Brandenburg for their guidance and patience during the cover design phase, and last but not least, Mark Chait, chief editor at Scribe Media, who turned out to be my light when I thought there was no light.

Our five children—Jairzinho, Jorzinho, Aimee, Antoine, and Angele—who have supported me unconditionally from the moment I first mentioned the idea of writing a book.

My sister, Gilian Martina, and my brother, George Martina, for their moral support.

And above all, my deepest gratitude to my queen Chantal Martina Seferina, an extraordinary, intelligent, disciplined woman who supported me and loved me unconditionally during this writing process that started on Sunday, May 7, 2023, when I wrote the first table of contents. Since that moment, it has been a beautiful journey of creation. When spirit calls, we have to respond.

Appendix

COURT OF FIRST INSTANCE OF CURAÇAO

Case numbers: CUR201903842/3843/3796/3844/3845/3846
    Judgment dated November 29, 2021
    The decision of court of first instance was:
    In the matter Stuart & Stevenson (affiliated company of the shareholder)

- Orders Ansary and Nina Ansary jointly and severally to pay to ENNIA Investments NAf 743,940,000, plus statutory interest from September 13, 2017, until the date of payment in full;

In respect of (dividend) payments

- Orders Ansary, Parman International, Nina Ansary, Andraous and Palm jointly and severally to pay to ENNIA Holding NAf 188,975,969, plus statutory interest from the time the separate (dividend) distributions were paid to Parman International until the day of payment in full.

In respect of donations

- Orders Ansary and Van Doorn jointly and severally to pay to
  ENNIA et al. the sum of NAf 10,574,500 and Ansary, Andraous
  and Palm further jointly and severally to pay to ENNIA Investments the sum of NAf 10,217,470, to be increased by the statutory
  interest from the time of payment of the donations in question
  until the day of payment in full;

In respect of counsel fees

- Orders Ansary and Andraous jointly and severally to pay to
  ENNIA Investments NAf 4,436,250 and Ansary further to pay
  NAf 1,700,000, to be increased by legal interest from the time
  of payment of the costs in question until the day of full payment;

In respect of salaries paid to persons who were not employed

- Orders Ansary and Van Doorn jointly and severally to pay ENNIA
  c.s. NAf 608,363, and Ansary furthermore to pay NAf 788,429 and
  Ansary, Andraous and Palm furthermore jointly and severally to
  pay NAf 4,237,392, to be increased by the legal interest from the
  moment of payment of the costs in question until the day of full
  payment;

In respect of the remuneration of members of the Supervisory
Board

- Orders Ansary and Van Doorn jointly and severally to pay to
  ENNIA c.s. NAf 315,770, and Ansary further to pay NAf 1,377,238,
  and Ansary and Nina Ansary further jointly and severally to pay
  NAf 436,440, and Ansary, Van Doorn and Nina Ansary further
  jointly and severally to pay NAf 1,737. 374, and Ansary and Nina
  Ansary furthermore jointly and severally to pay NAf 881,064, and

Ansary, Andraous, Palm and Nina Ansary furthermore jointly and severally to pay NAf 9,486,423, to be increased by legal interest from the time of payment of the relevant awards until the day of payment in full;

In respect of NetJets

- Orders Ansary to pay to ENNIA Investments NAf 5,522,781, and Ansary and Van Doorn furthermore jointly and severally to pay NAf 2,319,730, and Ansary, Andraous and Palm furthermore jointly and severally to pay NAf 19,879,770, to be increased by the legal interest from the moment of payment of the relevant awards until the day of full payment;

In respect of extrajudicial costs and litigation expenses

- Orders Ansary and Nina Ansary each to pay ENNIA et al. NAf 37,500 and each of the other defendants to pay NAf 9,000;
- Orders Ansary and Nina Ansary jointly and severally to pay the legal costs incurred on the part of ENNIA et al. assessed to date at NAf 15,000 for court registry fees, NAf 1,418.92 for court costs and NAf 100,000 for attorney's fees, plus subsequent costs of NAf 250 without service and NAf 400 with service, all amounts to be increased, in the event of non-payment, by statutory interest from the fifteenth day after the delivery of this judgment;

The Shareholder, Board of Supervisory Directors and Board of Managing Directors went to appeal against the judgment of the Court of First Instance.

COURT OF HIGH APPEAL OF CURAÇAO

Case numbers: CUR2022H00008/-H00009/-H00010/-H00011/-H00012/-H00013

Judgment dated September 12, 2023:

The decision of court of high appeal was:

The shareholder Ansary must pay at least about $140 million (250 million guilders) to this Curaçao insurance company, the Court ruled. That may possibly become more, depending on the outcome of a—new—valuation of Mullet Bay on St. Maarten. Because based on the valuation, the Court still has to assess whether the assets of ENNIA were sufficiently large to deem various (dividend) payments made to the shareholder (Parman International, owned by Ansary) from 2009 up to and including 2015 permissible; but also about the, according to the Central Bank CBCS, excessive compensation of the ex-supervisory directors and their travel and accommodation expenses, will be judged in more detail when the valuation report of the independent expert about Mullet Bay is available. In this interlocutory judgment, the Court refers the matter to the roll of October 24 next, when the parties can comment on what they believe to be a proper value. All this means that no final judgment has yet been rendered; thus delay, while the resolution of the ENNIA issue is dire, especially for the Country of Curaçao. Although the proposed ENNIA loan of 1.2 billion has not formally been taken into account for the claim, the verdict and what consequences it may have for addressing the financial problems—including the solvency deficit—at this large pension insurer were of course awaited.

The "amount of damages" for which Ansary and the other defendant former ENNIA directors have now been ordered by the Court on appeal is a lot lower than the amount of over a billion that was ruled by the Court of First Instance in November 2021. However, the liability may therefore increase even further after a thorough valuation of Mullet Bay is on the table and on the basis of that the Court will still make an additional ruling.

The parties (ENNIA on the one hand, in connection with the emergency regulation represented by the CBCS vs. Ansary cum suis on the other hand) are now first given the opportunity to comment on the expert to be appointed for a valuation of Mullet Bay in the relevant period and the wording of the question to be asked. Mullet Bay is so important to this case because the site on St. Maarten is one of ENNIA's largest assets.

Therefore, of overriding importance in the assessment is the (actual) value of Mullet Bay, the 49,000 square yard plot of land on St. Maarten that was contributed to ENNIA by Ansary at the time. However, Mullet Bay has been included in ENNIA's financial statements for increasingly high(er) amounts. The parties dispute the value of Mullet Bay.

The Court of Appeal finds that in the years in which the (dividend) distributions mentioned by ENNIA were made, Mullet Bay was erroneously included in the annual accounts for a value derived from two summary valuations by an appraiser," the Court of Appeal states in a press release "Therefore, it cannot be assumed that the (dividend) distributions made were made in accordance with the law and the articles of association."

It has been ruled that this claim is not assignable against former ENNIA director Gijsbert van Doorn and that the claim against Parman International and Nina Ansary—daughter of Hushang Ansary, respectively—is not assignable as a title of damages, but possibly (in part) on grounds of undue payment or unjust enrichment.

The Court cannot yet answer the question whether Ansary and others are liable for damages, because it cannot be ruled out that a proper valuation of Mullet Bay could have resulted in a (dividend) distribution of some amount. The three judges of the Court therefore find, first of all, that further expert information is necessary regarding the value that could reasonably have been attributed to Mullet Bay in the relevant years.

In an explanation to the media, the Court is already saying: "Should it turn out that in connection with overvaluation of Mullet Bay, ENNIA made more distributions to its shareholder than was legally and statutorily permissible, the Court will assess what amount must be (re) paid to ENNIA."

About the Author

GILBERT BERNARDO MARTINA was born on September 6, 1971, and raised on the island of Curaçao until age sixteen, when he departed for the Netherlands to study. He is the oldest of three children. Martina is married to Chantal Martina Mariana Johanna Seferina, and together they have five children: Jairzinho, Jorzinho, Aimee, Antoine, and Angele. Martina holds two master's degrees, one in chemical engineering and the other in business administration, from the University of Amsterdam and Webster University in Leiden, and has specialized in large change management programs, a post-graduate course from the Academy of Management, which is affiliated with the University of Groningen. Being part of a community with a strong history and diaspora in the transatlantic slave industry, a DNA ancestry test in March 2025 confirms that Martina's ancestral regions of 80 percent are from West Africa: 66 percent Benin and Togo; 10 percent Ivory Coast and Ghana; and 4 percent Central West Africa. This is the Martina lineage to the Shamanism of West Africa.

During the last four years that Martina worked for ENNIA (2013–2017), he launched a search for spiritual growth after suffering from lower-back pain and undergoing three surgeries. Through that stressful period, with many sleepless nights, Martina learned Transcendental Meditation and started to meditate twice a day. Alberto Villoldo and Marcela Lobos have also trained Martina at Four Winds Society, according to the ancient shamanic healing teachings of the Q'ero from Peru.

Martina is closing out his career as an executive director, during which he had to deal with social behavior driven by power and money and collective unconsciousness due to unhealthy minds and traumas from the past. Martina is launching a spiritual wellness center named The Blenchi Sanctuary, which he describes as "your place for shamanic healing energies and yoga." Blenchi is the local name for a hummingbird in Papiamentu. Hummingbirds always respond to the call of Great Spirit in search of the flowers with the best nectar in the world. They can travel 435 to 500 miles without worrying about food—quite a journey. Martina has been on quite a journey the last two and a half decades and has always responded to the call of Great Spirit, which has helped him to turn his wounds into sources of wisdom. Together with his queen Chantal, they will open this sanctuary to bring these teachings to every person who is open to receive it and transform their wounds into wisdom.

Healthy Minds, Healthy Nation is his personal transformative book to advocate spirituality in business and to be a spiritual leader to help everyone who is ready for the **spiritual journey of wake up, grow up, and show up**. It is a testimony about how we can maintain a calm mind and seek the light within when grief, trauma, and pain challenge our moral integrity. We can find our moral compass and inner light, and help others find theirs, so together we can change the world even in times of great turbulence.